LITERALLY,
THE BEST
LANGUAGE BOOK
EVER

LITERALLY, THE BEST LANGUAGE BOOK EVER

Annoying Words and Abused Phrases
You Should Never Use Again

PAUL YEAGER

A PERIGEE BOOK

A PERIGEE BOOK
Published by the Penguin Group
Penguin Group (USA) Inc.
375 Hudson Street, New York, New York 10014, USA
Penguin Group (Canada), 90 Eglinton Avenue East, Suite 700, Toronto, Ontario M4P 2Y3, Canada
(a division of Pearson Penguin Canada Inc.)
Penguin Books Ltd., 80 Strand, London WC2R 0RL, England
Penguin Group Ireland, 25 St. Stephen's Green, Dublin 2, Ireland (a division of Penguin Books Ltd.)
Penguin Group (Australia), 250 Camberwell Road, Camberwell, Victoria 3124, Australia
(a division of Pearson Australia Group Pty. Ltd.)
Penguin Books India Pvt. Ltd., 11 Community Centre, Panchsheel Park, New Delhi—110 017, India
Penguin Group (NZ), 67 Apollo Drive, Rosedale, North Shore 0632, New Zealand
(a division of Pearson New Zealand Ltd.)
Penguin Books (South Africa) (Pty.) Ltd., 24 Sturdee Avenue, Rosebank, Johannesburg 2196, South
Africa

Penguin Books Ltd., Registered Offices: 80 Strand, London WC2R 0RL, England

While the author has made every effort to provide accurate telephone numbers and Internet addresses
at the time of publication, neither the publisher nor the author assumes any responsibility for errors,
or for changes that occur after publication. Further, the publisher does not have any control over and
does not assume any responsibility for author or third-party websites or their content.

First edition: May 2008

Library of Congress Cataloging-in-Publication Data

Yeager, Paul.
   Literally, the best language book ever : annoying words and abused phrases you should never use
again / Paul Yeager.— 1st ed.
      p.   cm.
   Includes index.
   ISBN 978-0-399-53423-2
   1. English language—Errors of usage.   2. English language—Usage.   I. Title.
PE1460.Y39 2008.
428—dc22   2007046160

PRINTED IN THE UNITED STATES OF AMERICA

10   9   8   7   6   5   4   3   2   1

Most Perigee books are available at special quantity discounts for bulk purchases for sales promo-
tions, premiums, fund-raising, or educational use. Special books, or book excerpts, can also be created to fit specific needs. For details, write: Special Markets, Penguin Group (USA) Inc., 375 Hudson
Street, New York, New York 10014.

CONTENTS

INTRODUCTION

You're not safe from them anywhere. There are more of them today than there were yesterday, and there will be even more of them tomorrow. They're at work. They're at home. In fact, your parents, beloved grandparents, spouses, friends, and co-workers are all part of the problem, and if you're honest, you'll have to admit that you are, too.

I'm talking, of course, about language abuses—you know, the words, phrases, or expressions that make you want to stand up in a crowded room and desperately scream, "Is there a language expert in the house?" Most of us have felt that way at one time or another, and how could we not? Daily conversations are so overstuffed with words and phrases that are trite, trendy, grammatically incorrect, inane, outdated, or inappropriately informal that listening is sometimes impossible.

Instead of simply saying what we mean in our own words,

we now use prepackaged phrases, ineffective trendy expressions, and redundancies more than ever before. After hearing *reach out* at work ten times before lunch, I often wish that monks weren't the only group of people who were known to take a vow of silence. Instead of *thinking of a unique solution*, we must *think outside the box*. Instead of something being *finished*, it has to be **completely** *finished*. Nothing is merely *essential* any longer; it's **absolutely** *essential*.

We're also turning perfectly fine nouns into verbs at an unprecedented rate, with the result being many awkward nonwords being added to our vocabularies. Instead of *assigning a task to someone*, we're now *tasking someone with an assignment*. Instead of *having a dialogue with someone*, we're *dialoguing with him*. Instead of *making a transition*, we're *transitioning* from one thing to another. What's next? Instead of asking someone to *turn on a lamp* or *get a glass of water*, are we going to ask him to *lamp the room* or *glass some water*?

One of my personal favorites, and part of the inspiration for the title of this book, is the need for drama or, more accurately, melodrama in our language. It's not expressive enough to have *had a bad day*; it's got to be *the worst day ever*. It's not good enough to have *had a good birthday*; it has to be *the best birthday ever*. It's nearly impossible to go through an entire conversation without hearing at least one *worst ever*, *best ever*, *most ever*, *smallest ever*, *biggest ever*, *loudest ever*, *greatest ever*, *fastest ever*, *slowest ever*. . . .

Ever, ever, ever over and over and over again; tell me *that's* not annoying!

Of course, being annoyed isn't reason enough to write a book; otherwise, we'd all have to write books about all types of things. For instance, I'd also be writing books on reality television shows and using cell phones while driving. The reason for writing this particular book is that I wanted to make a serious attempt in a not completely serious way to help us communicate better.

Our personal use of language is as telling as a purple Mohawk haircut or body piercings or a tailored three-piece suit. Through our words, we have our best opportunity to let people know who we are and what we have to offer. That makes our language choices critical. When people follow the lead of others by using a prefabricated or trendy phrase rather than expressing thoughts and ideas in their own way, they are not only discarding their most basic form of individuality and creativity but are also training themselves to stop thinking. Mental laziness and playing follow the leader are good ways to ensure failure, while alertness and individuality are hallmarks of all successful people.

At work, when one person speaks in a less articulate manner than another person, the natural assumption is that the less articulate person is less prepared for the more challenging job. That's how one person is labeled as "a nice guy, but he's not too smart" while he struggles to advance, and another is labeled as "bright and can get the job done" and receives promotion after promotion. Studies have shown that people with good verbal skills receive higher wages than those with poor verbal skills.

Good communication is not just important at work. The

healthiest relationships with family and friends are those that deal with honest expressions of emotions, which is impossible when using clichés and not-so-clever quips. If a family member is disappointed about a job loss or if a friend is upset about a breakup, it's more respectful and helpful to deal with that specific problem than it is to reach into a bag of trite phrases and offer a blatantly dismissive *I wouldn't worry about that if I were you* or *Life isn't supposed to be easy* line. Imagine how ineffective that would be for you if you were the one going through a difficult time; *triteness* and *insincerity* are rarely considered synonyms for *loving* and *supportive*.

As far as starting new friendships, as we all know, the first impression is critical, and the first conversation is the most important part of generating that first impression. Many of us even remember the first time we had a conversation with someone who ultimately became a close friend. It's doubtful that any of us would like phrases such as *Awesome, dude* or *It's freakin' me out* or *I worked my ass off* to be part of our legacy—well, most of us anyway.

The entries in the book, more than 350 of them, have come from several sources. Many of them have come from my own observations, especially since my background as a writer, scientist (meteorologist), and managing editor of AccuWeather .com has honed my language and observation skills. Many of the entries have come from my wife, who is also a language and grammar expert (the finest I know) and who is also disturbed by the state of our discourse. In other words, she gets as annoyed about language as I do!

Other entries have come from willing participants, such as friends and family, who, upon learning that I was writing this book, would enthusiastically volunteer, "You *have* to include such and such. It drives me crazy when I hear that." Other entries have come from less-willing participants, such as professional athletes who average five *it is what it is* lines in every interview and the co-worker who has said *I'd tell you, but then I'd have to kill you* every time he's been asked a question since spy week aired on one of those all-movie channels back in the 1990s.

Although some standard grammar errors are included in the first four chapters—common grammar mistakes, redundancies, nouns incorrectly being used as verbs, and contrived and misused words and phrases—this book does not include only traditional grammar mistakes. That's what makes *Literally, the Best Language Book Ever* different from most traditional grammar books. Good grammar skills are important, but good communication is much more than merely avoiding grammar mistakes. That is the focus of Chapter 5 until the end of the book.

Many words and phrases in our current vocabulary simply don't make sense (Chapter 5), such as saying that *I could care less* when you, in fact, could not possibly care less or saying *I could be wrong* right before explaining why you think you're right. Good communication does not include using so many trendy phrases (Chapter 6) that the point of the discussion becomes secondary to the way it's being stated, which is inevitable when a bunch of *issues* and *concerns* are mixed in with a couple of *forward-thinkings* and some *blings*. Save the style points for the dance contest.

Many of the words and phrases we use at work (Chapter 7) are ineffective for myriad reasons, and we've now started to bring them home with us, giving them an entire second life of ineffectiveness. There are many stay-at-home mothers and fathers who now talk about the need for *efficiency* or *downtime* as if they were manning the production lines.

One of my favorite chapters is about expressions that we always think will make us sound witty and clever but actually do the opposite (Chapter 8). It's amazing how many times we repeat something that, when said to us, makes us think that the speaker is predictable and silly, such as asking *Are we having fun yet?* when things are going horribly wrong. What are we thinking!

Some of the common expressions that we rely on are hopelessly inarticulate (Chapter 9), dripping with insincerity (Chapter 10), or no longer relevant (Chapter 11). For example, tossing in a *Don't count your chickens before they hatch* hasn't added anything to a conversation since Aesop's milkmaid hung up her pail for the last time.

As pop culture has surpassed traditional culture, sports has become an increasingly important part of society. As a result, sports phrases (Chapter 12) are used more and more in daily conversations, and some of those phrases are too informal for most situations or have some of the problems that were outlined in the previous eleven chapters.

Finally, we all have what I would consider to be language pet peeves (Chapter 13), which are words, phrases, and expressions that are personally annoying, and I included some of mine (along with a few of my wife's—it's *my* book, and nepotism is alive and well) in this final chapter. As I do throughout the book, I try to give logical reasons for avoiding the words or phrases, but the entries in the last chapter either didn't fit neatly into one of the other chapters or were considered to be annoying enough to be a pet peeve. We all have pet peeves, and I invite you to share yours on my website, www.languageandgrammar .com. Maybe your entries will end up in my next book.

Before I finish the introduction, I want to make something clear: I am not setting myself up as some great language dictator. I doubt that you'll agree with every entry in the book, and that's not a problem. Just don't use them at my house.

My point is that, while many of the entries are, in fact, wrong without any doubt, some of the entries are more subjective. For example, a few of the words that I recommend avoiding will be found in dictionaries, especially online dictionaries, but we should remember that dictionaries are typically only a collection of commonly used words and phrases. In other words, an error used with enough regularity by enough people will land in a dictionary, and it's up to you to decide whether that makes it correct enough for you to include in your vocabulary. My position on the topic is clear.

I realize that we don't always need to be perfect in grammar, style, and articulation in order to communicate and have success in our lives and careers. It is my goal, however, to heighten the awareness of what we say so that we can better choose how we present ourselves.

It's a hope of mine that this book will help improve our language skills by providing accurate and useful information or, at least, by exposing the inanity of some of the things we say. More than anything, though, I hope this book will increase awareness of what we say so that we can begin to participate in, rather than glide through, our daily conversations. In other words, I want it to be *the best language book ever, literally.*

1

Wrong Answer; Please Try Again
GRAMMAR ERRORS

Fortunately, communicating well does not require being perfect at all times; however, some grammar mistakes are as painful to hear as a third-grade flute recital. In some cases, we've forgotten something basic that we had learned many years ago, but other mistakes are the result of what I call grammar peer pressure, meaning that we'd rather say something that we know is incorrect in order to sound like everyone else than say what we know is right.

You're not in high school any longer; stand out from the crowd by being correct.

a.m. in the Morning and p.m. in the Afternoon

In the morning means *in the a.m.*, and *a.m.* means *in the morning*, so they should not be said at the same time. Both *The meeting is at 9 a.m.* and *The meeting is at 9 in the morning* are correct; *The meeting is at 9 a.m. in the morning* is incorrect. The same obviously applies to *p.m. in the afternoon.*

That's not a revelation as much as a reminder, and it's also an easy way to monitor which people pay attention to what they're saying.

Everyone/Their

Everyone seems to make the mistake of pairing the singular *everyone* with the plural *their*, as is in *Is everyone ready for their grammar test?* rather than matching the singular *everyone* with the singular *his* or *her*, as in *Is everyone ready for his or her grammar test?*

This mistake probably started when people became more and more sensitive to the fact that men and women deserved to be treated equally, so rather than using the traditional *his* for the singular, it became common to use the non-gender term *their*. While that logic is certainly understandable, it's also the grammatical equivalent of the sound of fingernails on a chalkboard.

Other languages, such as Spanish and French, have allowed certain words and phrases that apply to both sexes to be defined as either masculine or feminine, so the old-fashioned way of defaulting to using the masculine singular term, *his*, to represent both is not the language equivalent of eliminating the Nineteenth Amendment, which gave women the right to vote. At the very least, we could use the singular term that best represents the group, whether it be *his* or *her*. Otherwise, just rewrite the sentence so that there is no confusion.

Firstly, Secondly, Lastly

In a basic sense, adverbs are words that answer the questions *How?, When?, Where?, How much?, Why?,* and to *What extent?* Adverbs often—*but not always*—end in *-ly*.

If you wanted to turn the verb *quick* into an adverb, an *-ly* would be added. *Quickly* answers the question of how was something done—*It was done quickly*—so it is an adverb. Words such as *first, second, third,* and *last* are already adverbs since they answer *when* was something done. *It was done first* or *It was done last*; there is no need to add the *-ly* in order to make these words adverbs; in fact, very few of us would ever add an *-ly* when using the words in this way (*It was done firstly*).

For some reason, however, it seems as though everyone adds the *-ly* to *first, second, third,* and *last* when listing events in a series as if there were magically something different when using the words as introductory phrases. *Firstly, I needed to determine the scope of the problem. Secondly, I thought of potential solutions. Thirdly, I talked to my boss about which solution he liked best. Lastly, I solved the problem.*

There's nothing magic about *-ly* for enumeration—unless poor grammar is magical.

Forecasted

The past tense of the word *forecast* is, well, *forecast*. *Forecasted* is often used as the past tense and is widely accepted. In fact, it will probably be found in every dictionary; however, this is another case of widespread misuse leading to widespread acceptance.

Cast can be used as a verb in a number of ways, such as *He cast* [threw] *the dice* or *She cast* [looked] *down at him* or *Light cast* [caused to fall] *a shadow in the room*; however, we would never use *casted* as the past tense in these instances.

Logically, then, why would *forecasted* be the past tense of *forecast*? That doesn't make sense. The problem, most likely, is that we're all so used to adding *-ed* to make the past tense of so many words in our language that we extend that rule to words to which it doesn't apply. Language doesn't work like the local supermarket; there are no buy-one-get-one-free deals: one word, one past tense.

Use *forecast* as the past tense of *forecast*. It's the same with *broadcast*, *telecast*, and *simulcast*.

It Don't Make Much Sense

The difference between *don't* and *doesn't* is, of course, basic grammar; however, I've heard enough otherwise articulate people say *don't* when *doesn't* would be correct, such as in *It don't make much sense*, to include it here.

We all know that *It do not make much sense* doesn't make much sense, so the error most likely comes from a temporary memory lapse of what the contraction *don't* actually means.

It's Me

We were all, with any luck, taught in grade-school English class that *It's I* is correct. The reason that it should be *It's I* instead of *It's me* is that any time you have the verb *is*, the first-person singular pronoun that follows should be *I*, not *me*. Some of us have heard the mistaken *It's me* so often that we're now confused, which is understandable. The rest of us, however, understand that *It's I* is correct but choose to say *It's me* instead because *It's I* is considered formal and stuffy.

It might be hard to believe, but it's true—many of us would rather be wrong and sound like everyone else than be correct and perceived as something we don't like. *Me thinks* that says a lot about how insecure most people are. By the way, *Me thinks* is as incorrect as *It's me*.

A non-grammar note about the phrase *It's me*: It never makes sense to say it to another person, whether it be on voice mail, an answering machine, at the front door, or in response to the question *Who's there?* Either the person knows you well enough so that it's not necessary to say *It's me* or more information is needed for the person to know who it is, which could be handled by simply saying *It's Paul* rather than *It's me*.

I've Went . . .

Saying *I've went* rather that *I've gone*, as in *I've went to that movie three times* rather than *I've gone to that movie three times*, is incorrect. This has to do with the difference between the past tense and the past participle being complicated because the verb (*to go*) is an irregular verb.

If all you want to know is that you should never use *have* (or the contraction, such as *I've*) with *went* (use *gone* instead), then move on to the next entry. But if you want to listen to me struggle through the explanation, then keep reading!

The present perfect tense is used to describe something that started in the past and is still true. *I have been sitting here for three days. She has taken the dog for a walk. They have walked ten miles so far today.* The present perfect tense consists of *have/has* and the past participle of the verb. In this case, for the verb *to go*, the past tense is *went* and the past participle is *gone*. The present perfect tense, then, is *have/has gone*, which is what we're aiming for in this case.

I Wish I Was

There are two ways to quickly clear a room—yell *Fire!* and hope that a close relative has bail money available or start talking about grammar terms such as present perfect or conjunctive adverb and be branded as boorish. Rather than dry, eye-glazing grammar rules, sometimes a quick little tip will suffice.

Whenever you wish things were different from the way they actually are, use *were* rather than *was*, as in *If I were rich, then I'd finally be happy* rather than *If I was rich, then I'd finally be happy*.

That's all you need to know. But if you want the reason, it has to do with the subjunctive mood, which is, according to *Merriam-Webster's Collegiate Dictionary*, Eleventh Edition, "a verb form . . . that represents a denoted act or state not as a fact but as contingent or possible or viewed emotionally." In other words, if it didn't happen, but you wish it had, then use *were*.

It's the same with *had*, which is the past subjunctive form of the verb *to have* (*did* is the past tense of *do*, and *had* is the past subjunctive of the verb *to have*). If you use *wish* with a past tense or if you're describing something that you wish had happened in the past but didn't, then use *had* rather than using either *did* or just the simple past tense of the verb. For example, you would say *I wish I had learned more about grammar in school* rather than *I wish I learned more about grammar in school* or *I wish I did learn more about grammar in school*. You would also say *If I had learned more, then I would be smarter*, not *If I learned more, then I'd be smarter*.

Speaking of wishes, I almost wish I hadn't started to try to explain the subjunctive.

Less Things

Fewer should be used when dealing with anything that you can count, such as *I have fewer apples in my kitchen than you have in yours*. Perhaps I have three while you have six.

Less should be reserved for things that cannot be measured by number, such as *I have less water in my canteen than you have in yours*, or for something of a smaller degree, such as *I have less patience for language errors now than I did when I was younger*.

Like

No one keeps statistics on such matters, so I can't prove it; however, I believe that the frequency of use of the word *like* has increased more than nearly any other word in our language during the past couple of decades. Part of it is the Valley girl–like tendency to *like* throw the word into *like* every sentence a couple of times. Can we stop that?

The other increase in the usage of *like* has more to do with a grammar error. In nearly every instance by nearly every person, the word *like* is now used instead of the grammatically correct *as if* or *as though*. For example, *It appears as if it will rain tomorrow* is correct, whereas *It appears like it will rain tomorrow* is incorrect. *As if* can have—and should have—an independent clause after it; *like* should not. In the example, *It will rain tomorrow* is an independent clause, so *as if* is the correct choice. In *It looks like a group of clouds that has no definite shape but is threatening just the same*, everything after *like*, even though it is a long clause, is not an independent clause; there is no verb for the subject, so using *like* is correct.

Like gets enough airtime with proper usages, which include expressing affection (*I like her*) or as part of a simile (*He looks like death*), so we don't need to invent new ways to use it.

Literally

Literally is one of the most misused words in our poor, abused language. *Literally* means that what's been described has actually happened, whereas *figuratively* means that a figure of speech has been used in order to create a desired effect. For example, *I literally sat down in front of the computer and started to type* and *I figuratively could die for a piece of cheesecake* are both correct statements.

If you were so scared that you *literally jumped through the roof,* then there'd better be a hole in your roof and a bandage on your head. If it were so hot that you could *literally cook an egg on the sidewalk,* then I'll take mine sunny-side up—and don't forget the bacon.

Me and You

Saying *me and you* (or *me and my family, me and them,* and so on) is *always* incorrect. There are two possible errors. The first is the order. Nothing personal, but *you* (meaning *me* when speaking) should always be listed last. For example, saying *The waiter asked you and me to pay our check* is correct, whereas *The waiter asked me and you to pay our check* is incorrect.

The other potential error is when *you and I* should be used instead of *you and me.* The simple rule is that if you can substitute the pronoun *us,* then use *you and me.* *John asked **you and me** to keep an eye on his pit bull* this weekend is correct because *John asked **us** to keep an eye on his pit bull* is also correct. If you can substitute the word *we,* then use *you and I.* For example, *John asked if **you and I** could watch his pit bull this weekend* is correct because *John asked if **we** could watch his pit bull this weekend* is also correct.

Overuse of Prepositions

It is sometimes difficult to hear the truth, but we have to understand the truth in order to grow, so here goes: We live in a preposition-obsessed society. I know it was difficult to hear—it was difficult for me to say, as well. If need be, take a minute to pull yourself together before continuing.

The major abuse of the preposition falls into two major categories: (1) adding *up*, *down*, *on*, or *off* when not necessary and (2) using two prepositions when one will suffice.

We love to say *Heat **up** the pan* rather than *Heat the pan* or that *The iron cools **down*** or *cools **off*** rather than *It cools*. We say that *Things are looking **up*** rather than *Things are looking better*. We say *We're moving **on*** rather than *We're taking the next step*. We *point **out*** mistakes rather than *calling them to our attention*. I could go *on* and *on* and *on* . . . wait, I mean, could continue, but you get the point.

The second problem—using two prepositions in a row—sounds as disharmonious as the string section of an orchestra tuning instruments before a classical concert. Weather forecasters, especially on the twenty-four-hour-per-day cable networks, are the worst abusers. Cold fronts are always *moving **up into*** a region; rain is *moving **over toward*** a state; a high pressure system is *moving **on off*** the coast (my favorite since *on* and *off* are opposites). Occasionally, the meteorologist will hit the rare triple preposition, such as *Showers are moving **on over into*** a region. That's true talent.

Perhaps the two errors are related. We've become so accustomed to using prepositions where they're not needed that when we actually do need one, we just throw another one into the sentence.

As a general rule, use *on*, *off*, *up*, and *down* only when other words won't work, which usually means when referring to directions and light switches, and never put two prepositions back-to-back. These are easy ways to break our preposition addiction—and sound more intelligent.

Possibly Might/Chance That It Might

Uncertainty is a part of life, which is why we have words such as *possibly*, *might*, and *chance*; however, it *might possibly* be that using too many uncertain terms together *could perhaps* make a person sound too wishy-washy—*maybe*. At least that's what I think. Don't you agree? Besides, using more than one of the three words *possibly*, *might*, and *chance* in the same sentence is superfluous.

Use either *I might go to the store tomorrow* or *I will possibly go to the store tomorrow*, but don't say *I possibly might* (or *could possibly* or *perhaps might* or *maybe could*) *go to the store tomorrow*. Also, avoid the double uncertainty even if the words are separated. For instance, instead of *There is a chance that it might rain tomorrow*, say *There is a chance that it will rain tomorrow* since the uncertainty applies to whether it will rain, not to whether it *might* rain.

Should Of

Most people understand the correct usage of the words *have* and *of*, so their misuse—such as saying *I should of gone to the store while I was out* instead of *I should have gone to the store while I was out*—is generally a pronunciation problem or sloppiness. The contraction *should've* sounds like *should of*.

As we've seen, though, innocent errors often spread throughout the language more quickly than a runny nose through a daycare center, so mind your *of*s and *have*s.

So with a Negative

The word *so* has many uses, and it's probably one of the most commonly used words in the English language. In fact, it's used *so* (see what I mean?) often that we don't need to invent ways to use it even more, as in using *so* with *not* for the purpose of emphasis.

You don't have to sound like a Valley girl in order to emphasize something negative. I have a bold idea: Just say what you mean in a measured, straightforward manner. Instead of saying *I'm so not going*, say *I'm definitely not going* or, more simply, *I'm not going*. Instead of saying *It's so not true*, try *It's definitely not true* or *It's not true*. Instead of saying *It's so not beautiful*, try *Damn, that's ugly*.

Stupidest

The irony is never lost on me when a person says that someone else is the *stupidest* or has done the *stupidest* thing since the truly stupid thing is using the non-word *stupidest* in the first place.

It's not always as simple as merely adding an *-er* or *-est* to an adjective to increase the quantity or degree of the word (the comparative and superlative forms). In some cases, you must use *more* and *most* in advance of the root word to create the desired effect. Let's use the word *hectic* as an example. *Hecticer* and *hecticest* sound ridiculous, but *more hectic* and *most hectic* are correct. It's the same with *stupid*. It's always *more stupid* and *most stupid*, not *stupider* and *stupidest*.

There Is a Lot

There is a lot of grammar mistakes—I mean, *There are a lot of grammar mistakes*—that can be easily forgiven. Either simple confusion has led to the error or overuse of a non-word has given people the impression that the "word" in question actually *is* a word; however, I do not understand the rapidly growing trend over the past couple of years for people to combine the singular *there is* or *there's* with something plural, as in *There is (there's) a lot of reasons for making this mistake* rather than the correct *There are a lot of reasons for making this mistake*.

It *are* a trend that we need to stop.

These Type

Saying the incorrect *these type*, such as *These type of problems*, rather than the correct *These types of problems*, seems to be occurring more and more frequently. It's the same as the "Everyone/Their" error discussed earlier in this chapter; match the plural *types* with the plural *these*, and keep the singular *this* for the singular *type*.

Unhealthy Food

The misuse of the words *healthy* and *healthful* reminds me of my days as a weather forecaster, especially when referring to air quality. Something that is *unhealthful* doesn't promote good health, so *unhealthful* air quality is air that is below a standard that is considered good for our lungs. *Unhealthy* means lacking in health, so *unhealthy* air, if there were such a thing, would be air that was sick—perhaps the air has asthma.

It's the same for anything else, including food. *Unhealthful food* is food that will not promote good health, such as chili cheese fries, while *unhealthy food* is food that is lacking in health, such as a blackened banana.

I understand that common misuse of these words has resulted in acceptance in some circles, but those are not *grammatically healthful* circles. Or are they not grammatically *healthy* circles?

Years Experience

It always feels good to undo a few mistakes of the past, so with that in mind, please read the following carefully: of, of, of, of, of, of, of, of, of, of, of, of, of, of, of, and of.

That makes up for the last sixteen times that someone has said (or written) *years experience*, such as in *She has seven years experience as an accountant* rather than the correct *She has seven years of experience as an accountant*. While it's possible that some people are actually saying *years' experience* (with the apostrophe), which is called the genitive case, I highly doubt it since most don't know what the genitive case is. If you don't believe me, then ask a few people at work tomorrow to explain the genitive case—I know I will. The use of the genitive case in *years' experience* is still somewhat debatable but is widely accepted. But you can never go wrong with the *always* grammatically correct *years of experience*.

Although conversations rarely come with apostrophes included, I believe there are two possible reasons for the *years experience* trend, including laziness (just skipping the of) and as an overflow of the *it's all good* generation's trend of skipping prepositions (*I'm done my homework* instead of *I'm done with my homework*).

Regardless of the reason, we all need to do our part to stop it. Say it with me: of, of, of, of, of, of, of, of, of, of, of, and of!

2

Play It Again, Sam
ERRORS OF REDUNDANCY
AND REPETITION

So little thought is given to what we say that our everyday conversations are full of repetition and redundancy. Common phrases, since they're used so often, are never examined before being uttered, so any redundancy easily becomes part of the language. The result is often that two words are paired without any thought to their superfluous nature, such as *blazing inferno*.

At other times, we're in such a rush to get our words out quickly—for fear that the opportunity to speak will be lost in our fast-paced world, which is full of people with short attention spans—that we don't give our brains enough time to translate what we're thinking into a coherent phrase.

At other times, we're in such a rush to get our words out quickly—for fear that the opportunity to speak will be lost in our fast-paced world, which is full—wait, now I'm repeating myself.

12 Midnight and 12 Noon

The *12* part is already included in the *midnight* or *noon*, so there is no need to say both (*12 midnight* or *12 noon*). It's either *midnight* or *noon* or *12 a.m.* or *12 p.m.*, but it is always safe to stick to *midnight* and *noon* since some people get confused with a.m. and p.m.

For the record, the *m* in *a.m.* and *p.m.* stands for *meridian*, which means *midday*. Since *ante* means *before* and *post* means *after*, *a.m.* means *morning* and *p.m.* means *afternoon*; therefore, saying *a.m. in the morning* and *p.m. in the afternoon* both mean that you spend too much time repeating yourself.

Absolutely Essential

By definition, *essential* means *absolutely necessary*, so by definition, then, it's *absolutely necessary*, or *essential*, that *absolutely* is not essential in the phrase *absolutely essential*.

Added/Extra Bonus

Bonuses are *extra* or are *added* to what was already expected, so it makes no sense to modify *bonus* with either *added* or *extra*. Technically, if you received one bonus and got a second, then saying *extra bonus* might be fine, but how often does that happen? One bonus is more than most of us can expect in this economy.

And Also

And also is so obvious that I almost didn't include it in this book; however, it's said too often to be ignored. Since *and* and *also* both obviously mean the same thing, just pick one, not both.

The mistake probably occurs because the word *and* is so often used as a space filler that we tend to forget that it means *in addition to*, so we use the word *also* without realizing the repetition.

Anecdotal Story

An *anecdote* is a story, just as a banana is a fruit. Saying *anecdotal story* would be like saying a *banana fruit* rather than just saying *banana*.

ATM Machine

The *M* in *ATM* stands for *machine* (automated teller machine); therefore, it is redundant to say *ATM machine*.

Best Ever

Ask a six-year-old what kind of a birthday she had, and she's likely to respond with *I had the best birthday ever*. How adorable; the child was so excited about balloons and cake that she didn't realize the mistake.

Adults, however, should notice the redundancy and avoid it. *Best* means *never better*. Therefore, if someone were to say that *I had the best ever vacation* or *I had the best vacation ever*, then he may as well say *I've never ever had a better vacation*, which might sound adorable if he were still six years old.

Best ever is certainly not the only abuse. The same redundancy exists for *greatest ever, most ever, least ever, worst ever*, and so on (for more, see "Ever," in Chapter 6).

Blazing Inferno

Certain words are used together so often that they've almost become one word. Rarely is the word *inferno* mentioned without the word *blazing* preceding it. Since no *inferno* can be anything but a *blazing* one, it's redundant; and if the two words are combined for dramatic effect—it's not just an *inferno* but it's a ***blazing inferno***—then the drama is lost since that's how it's always said.

Trite has never been confused with *dramatic*.

Brief Summary

A *summary* is a condensed (meaning shortened) version of a larger piece of information; it should be *brief* by definition, so avoid saying *brief summary*.

But Nevertheless

In this instance, *but* means *on the contrary*, and *nevertheless* means *in spite of*. Unless *on the contrary in spite of* makes sense, *but nevertheless* should be avoided.

Close Proximity

Proximity means *near* or *close to*, so *close proximity* is redundant. This is a good example of our tendency to repeat what we often hear without thinking about the meaning of the phrase; the redundant *close proximity* is often said, but the equally redundant *near proximity* is rarely, if ever, said.

Combine Together

Unless *combine apart* makes sense, adding *together* to *combine* is not necessary. *Combine* already means *to bring together*.

Completely Finished

Finished means that it's done. It's time to stop. There's nothing left to do. In other words, it's been *completed*. Adding the word *completely*, as in *completely finished*, doesn't make it more so; in fact, it means there's one more word to get to before the finish.

Completely Surrounded

An island is *surrounded* by water—it has water on all sides; saying that it is *completely surrounded* does not add to the description since there is only one way to be surrounded, and that is *completely*.

On the other hand, a peninsula, such as Florida, has water on three sides—that is, it's not *surrounded* by water. It's also not *partially surrounded* by water since it would also make no sense to say that it's *partially completely surrounded by water*.

Consensus of Opinion

Consensus of opinion, a phrase that is particularly popular in meetings, doesn't make sense since *consensus* already means that everyone has agreed to a position, which would be the official *opinion* of the group.

If that's the level of intelligence of those who attend meetings, then I'm even more pleased that I canceled all of mine (see "Postpone Until Later," later in this chapter).

Continue to Remain

I am going to *continue* on my quest to talk about language, or I'm going to *remain* on my quest to talk about language. Not even I, an author of a book on the subject, however, should *continue to remain* on my quest since it's redundant.

Cooperate Together

There is only one way to *cooperate,* and that is with someone else. It's impossible to *cooperate by yourself* or *cooperate separately,* so there is no need to add *together* to the word *cooperate.* It's already part of the existing definition.

Déjà Vu All Over Again

The phrase *déjà vu all over again* has been attributed to Yogi Berra, who became famous for using the English language in the same way that a heavy-metal guitarist might play the harp.

This was a cute, redundant play on words at the height of its career (and Yogi's, for that matter), but talk about playing past your prime. . . . I doubt even Yogi still says it.

Duplicate Copy

A *copy* had better be a *duplicate*; otherwise, it's not a *copy*. *Duplicate copy* is redundant; use either one but not both.

Final Conclusion

A *conclusion* means the end. It's over. There isn't any more. In other words, it's *final*. Adding the word *final* doesn't make it any more so; in fact, similar to the expression *completely finished* (see earlier in this chapter), *final conclusion* means that there's one more word to get through before arriving at the *conclusion*.

Follow After

To *follow* means to come *after*, as in *follow* the leader, not *follow after* the leader.

Free Gift

The beauty of a *gift* is that it's *free*; otherwise, it wouldn't be a *gift*. It could be a loan or a purchase or a trade, but it cannot be a *gift* unless it's *free*.

The phrase *free gift*, ironically, usually means a gift with strings attached. At the cosmetics counter of any department store, there is usually at least one huge sign that says *free gift*, with small print that adds *with every $50 purchase* that isn't legible until the customer is within harassment range of a sales associate.

Go ahead. Try to get the *gift* for *free*. I've never had any luck.

Heavy Downpours

Thunderstorms will bring heavy downpours. If I had a weather-vane for every time I heard that one, then . . . The only possible reason for indicating that *downpours will be heavy* would be if *downpours* could be anything else, such as *light*, which they cannot.

Hot Water Heater

If *hot water* came into homes from the water company, then none of us would need *hot water heaters*; instead, we would need *hot water coolers* so that we could take a shower without getting burned. Since the water is cool when it arrives at the house, we need a *cool water heater*, which is more typically referred to as a *water heater*.

Intentional Fraud

If a businessman changes invoices prior to mailing in a deliberate attempt to overcharge for his services, then it's *fraud*. It's no accident; he chose to cheat. On the other hand, if he accidentally enters the wrong numbers into the computer and overcharged clients, then it's not deliberate, and it's not fraud.

All *fraud* is *intentional*, so *intentional fraud* is repetitious.

IRA Account

The *A* in *IRA* stands for *account* (individual retirement account); therefore, *IRA account* is redundant.

Irregardless

This is a rarity—a single word redundancy!

The prefix *ir-* means *not*. An **ir**responsible person is one who is *not* responsible. Regardless means *without regard*. *Irregardless*, then, means *not without regard*, and if we apply our typical rule of a double negative resulting in a positive, *irregardless* would then mean *with regard*, which is the opposite of what we intend with *irregardless*.

Regardless is the only correct word.

Join Together

Join means to *put together*, so *to join together* means *to put together together*, which is as redundant as sealing, gluing, and *stapling* an envelope closed.

Long Litany

A *litany* of something is a *long*, tedious account, such as *the workers had a litany of complaints about their work environment.* Notice that the word *long* is already included in the definition; adding *long* to *litany* is analogous to adding the word *repetitious* to *redundant*, such as *long litany is a repetitious, redundant phrase.*

Mass Exodus

The phrase *mass exodus* is another classic example of not paying attention when speaking. If we were to think for a moment, then we would realize that an *exodus* is already a *mass* movement of people. A *mass exodus*, then, would be a *mass mass movement of people*.

Mutual Agreement

An agreement means that more than one party is involved, and all accept the terms of the *arrangement*—that is, *they agree*. A *mutual agreement*, on the other hand, is one that is *agreeable* to all parties involved. Wait a minute. That's not the other hand—that's the same hand. Both mean that the arrangement is *agreeable* to all parties; therefore, *mutual agreement* is redundant.

Perhaps *mutual disagreement* would be more acceptable: The parties agree (*mutual*) that they don't agree (*disagreement*). In fact, that would be a much better way of saying *we'll have to agree to disagree* since that phrase, as well, is overused.

New Development

The words *new* and *development* are said together as if they were one word, *newdevelopment*. We must have forgotten that when something *develops*, it wasn't there before, so it's *new*. Adding the word *new* doesn't make it any more so.

The only possible exception is when *development* is being used as a reference for a group of homes; in that case, there can be a *new development* across the street from the older one.

Over-Exaggerate

To *exaggerate* means to overstate, as in *Bobby exaggerated his sickness so his mother would allow him to stay home from school*. Adding an *over-* to it, as in *over-exaggerate*, does not add to the *exaggera-*

tion, but it does add to the number of people who use a word that makes no sense.

Partially Naked

As the old saying goes, *We're all naked under our clothes*; however, we are never *partially naked* in any situation. *Naked* means completely without clothing. For the sake of convenience or out of laziness, it has become popular to describe a person who is *partially clothed* as *partially naked*; however, even wearing one lonely, little sock means that a person is not naked. The person might be embarrassed, but he's not naked.

PIN Number

Similar to *ATM machine* and *IRA account* (see earlier in this chapter), the *N* in *PIN* stands for *number* (personal identification number); therefore, *PIN number* is redundant.

Postpone Until Later

I don't mind meetings in theory; however, since nothing has ever been accomplished in any meeting, I have no use for them. That's why I'm going to *postpone all of my meetings until earlier*.

What do you mean I can't postpone them until earlier? If I can *postpone them until later*, then it's only logical that I can postpone them until earlier. Oh, that's right. *Postpone* already means *until later*, so neither phrase—*postpone until later* nor *postpone until earlier*—makes any sense. One is redundant, and the other is impossible.

In that case, I'll just have to *cancel* all of my meetings.

Qualified Expert

An *expert* is someone who has some level of special skill that makes the person *qualified*. I would imagine that this started as a sort of marketing gimmick—not only do we have an *expert* but he's a *qualified expert*; however, a quick search on the Internet reveals how widespread this redundancy has become: My search found about 20,000 references.

I hope that doesn't mean we also have 20,000 *unqualified experts* out there!

Revert Back

Revert means to *return to a previous condition*, such as *revert to my old ways*. In other words, it means to go *backward* in some way; therefore, the word *back* is not needed in *revert back*.

Seriously Consider

Technically, to *consider* anything means that it is thought about carefully, so *seriously consider* means to *seriously think about it carefully*, which, of course, makes no sense.

The misuse of the phrase, though, is understandable in the sense that there are degrees of consideration. For instance, the decision to buy a new car and the decision about the best course of treatment for a serious illness both require consideration, but one is deserving of more serious consideration than the other.

That distinction might be acceptable, but generally speaking, the phrase *seriously consider* is just thrown around without any thought whatsoever and should, therefore, be avoided.

Small/Large in Size

Unless otherwise stated, it is assumed that *small* and *large* are referring to size, so it's not necessary to include the word *size*. For instance, *the grapefruit is small* makes more sense than *the grapefruit is small in size*. When describing something that is not physical, such as stature, it might be better to use the word *size* to emphasize the comparison, as in *he might be small in size but not in stature*.

Some But Not All

If you have *some* of a thing, then it means that you do not have *all* of it, and when you do not have *all* of something, then you have *some* of it; therefore, *some but not all* is repetitious.

So/Very Unique

If something is *unique*, then it is already one of a kind. Adding a modifier to make it sound even more *unique*, such as *so unique* and *very unique*, is mere repetition. It would be similar to saying *my collection is very one of a kind*.

Terrible Tragedy

Perhaps we have started to use the word *tragedy* to describe events that aren't so much tragic as disappointing, such as *The presentation I gave today was a tragedy*, and perhaps that's why we've felt the need to add the adjective *terrible* to describe a true *tragedy*.

It's more likely that we've just become accustomed to saying *terrible tragedy* and don't notice the obvious redundancy, which is that all true *tragedies* are *terrible* by definition.

Totally/Completely Free Checking

Check for attached strings on this one, but *totally free* or *completely free checking* is, in fact, usually *free*.

What's odd is that the bank, which makes interest on our money, charges us to get access to our money (through the ATM), charges ridiculous fees for bounced checks, and loans our money for a much higher interest rate than they give for savings accounts, would consider providing one service for free as doing us a big favor. That's why banks have to make such a big deal out of it; otherwise, no one would believe it. It's not just *free*, which means there are no charges, but it's *completely free*. It's *totally free*. We mean it!! It's *free, free, free*!!

If something is *free*, then there is no need to add any modifiers. And if it's not *free*, then don't try to pretend that it is.

True Fact/Honest Truth

We have become so accustomed to drawing subtle lines when communicating, that in many instances, a "fact" might be presented in such a way that it's not actually true. Or the *truth* might actually be something that is technically "true" but deliberately misleading.

If we did less of that nonsense, then we might not need redundant phrases like *true fact* and the *honest truth*.

Tweak It a Little

Tweak, of course, means to *make a minor adjustment*, as in *I'm going to tweak the recipe to make it my own*. Perhaps oregano was substituted for basil and canned tomatoes for fresh. It's a minor adjustment; no one would even notice.

Tweak it a little, then, would mean *make a minor, little adjustment*. If you're only going to change it *that* little, then don't even bother.

Unexpected Surprise

You can't possibly have an *expected surprise*—they're **all** *unexpected*; otherwise, it wouldn't be a *surprise*. Just say that the party was *unexpected* or that it was a *surprise*, not that it was an *unexpected surprise*.

Vast Majority

Vast majority is technically not redundant since there are varying degrees of a majority. A *simple majority* might include as little as one more than the minority, and a *vast majority* is considerably larger but still not the complete group; however, *vast* and *majority* are typically paired without any consideration of the numbers involved in a specific case—actually without any thought whatsoever. It should, therefore, be avoided.

Visible to the (Naked) Eye

We never say that something is *audible to the ear* or *audible to the naked ear*, but we often feel the need to explain that something is *visible to the naked eye* or *visible to the eye*. Unless we start to see in another way or corrective lenses start producing microscopic vision, adding the words *to the eye* is not necessary.

3

Verbification
NOUNS BEING INCORRECTLY
USED AS VERBS

This chapter probably has more debatable entries than any other in the book since nouns have been turned into verbs for generations and generations. Some are firmly entrenched in our language and are accepted by most people; others are on the way to becoming widely accepted, but grammarians still argue about their validity.

There are many others that have been invented in just the past couple of years—when turning nouns into verbs has surpassed baseball as the national pastime. While it seems to be done as a way of trying to sound more intelligent or authoritative, it rarely works out that way. The result is a world full of trendy non-words that turn the focus of the conversation from the point of the discussion to the awkwardness of the speaker.

In other words, it's just plain wrong.

Accent

We all know that an *accent mark* dictates which syllable to stress in a word and that it's acceptable to *accent* a particular syllable. In that sense, *accent* is both a noun and a verb.

An *accent* is also something that emphasizes or highlights, such as *The room was beige with red accents*; however, it's wrong to use *accent* as a verb in that way. In other words, *The lighting accents the size of his nose* and *The red accents the otherwise beige room* should both be avoided.

In the first example, the correct word would be *accentuates* (*The lighting accentuates the size of his nose*); in the second example, it's just another misused noun.

Access

It has become fashionable to use the word *access* as a verb, such as *I accessed the records from the computer*; however, *access* is definitely a noun that is incorrectly being used as a verb. In other words, it has been misused often enough so that people have started to believe that it is a verb, and it has started to be included in some dictionaries.

Use *The computer has given me access to the records* instead. Maybe if we all just commit to using it correctly, we will have *access* to one fewer "verbified" noun.

Antiquing

An *antique* is something old; if this noun were to be used as a verb, such as *antiquing*, then it would most likely mean *to turn something old*. It certainly wouldn't mean *the process of collecting old things*, which is what the noun-turned-verb seems to mean.

Architect

We all know an *architect* is what the George Costanza character on *Seinfeld* sometimes pretended to be, but more important, it's the person who designs or creates something, typically a building. The word has been around since the middle of the sixteenth century.

What is a much more recent creation is the use of the word as a verb to mean the act of creating or designing something, such as *He architected our new business plan*. It may be used with the belief that the new usage sounds more impressive than the old way of speaking (*He is the architect of our new business plan*), but since the word offends the senses of those who understand language, it leaves the impression of false importance. In fact, that's the problem with many of the nouns that are turned into verbs.

Chair

This is undoubtedly one entry with which some will disagree; however, logic is on my side. A *chair* is something that a person sits on, and *chairs* were around long before the word was ever used as a verb, as in *He chairs the committee on making substandard words acceptable.*

We needed to invent a title for someone who headed a committee since committees came along long after *chairs*, and *chairman* was a fine choice, as were the gender-sensitive terms *chairwoman* and *chairperson*; however, we certainly did not need to turn the word *chair* into a verb since we had ways of saying that someone is the *chairperson* of a committee, such as *He's the chairperson of the committee.*

If we decide to consider *chair* to be a verb, how far away are we from saying that *I chaired by the fire* rather than *I sat on the chair beside the fire*?

Conference

A *conference* is when two or more people *confer* about something. For example, *Parents and teacher confer about a child's school performance at a parent–teacher conference.* You'll notice that example contains both a verb, *confer*, and a noun, *conference*.

Since the words *confer* and **confer**ence are so obviously related, it is pretty clear that they were intended to be two different forms of the same word. *Confer* means to consult with others, so there is certainly no need for *conference* to be used to say the same thing.

Saying *I conferenced with my child's teacher about his performance* means that the teacher should give you a poor grade in basic English.

Dialogue

A *dialogue* is something—a conversation; it's not something that's done. *I had a dialogue with my colleagues about the new project* is correct; *I dialogued with my colleagues about the new project* is incorrect. It's like the word *lamp. Please turn on the lamp so that I can read* is correct; *Lamp the room so that I can read* is incorrect—and silly.

Drywalling

As we all know, a noun is a thing, and it's hard to imagine a more solid noun than a wall, most of which are now made out of *drywall*. It's not moving—at least not without power tools, a sledgehammer, or an angry teenager—however, there has been a trend by recent construction workers and home renovators (professionals and do-it-yourselfers) to try to move the usage of *drywall* from a noun to a verb, such as *I plan on drywalling the basement this weekend.*

Leave the language construction to the professionals.

DVR'd

VCRs have been used in nearly every household in this country since the 1980s, and, typically, people have said that they've *recorded* or *taped* a program, which makes perfect sense. I'm happy to say that I've never heard anyone say that they've *VCR'd* anything.

For the new generation, it's the DVR rather than the VCR, and I often hear people say that they *DVR'd* something. That represents a major generational difference. Not only is it common to turn nouns into verbs but it also might soon become a trend to turn acronyms into verbs. TiVo is the name of a company, so saying *TiVo'd* isn't any better. (See also "Google It," later in this chapter.)

Gift

Whenever I hear the word *gift* being used as a verb, as in *I'm going to gift this set of candles*, I think of the episode of *Seinfeld* when the characters invented the process of *re-gifting*. For them, *re-gifting* meant passing off an unwanted gift to someone else as a new gift. That was an active process, meaning that the word was a verb. For the rest of us, it meant a few laughs and perhaps tacit permission to transform another noun into a verb.

For those of us who want to speak well, the laugh is on us!

Google It

I have never understood who gets to invent words and why, but I'm guessing that most words have been invented because of a need to express a new idea or as a name for a new discovery or invention. Laziness or convenience should not be on the list. Of course, that's only part of the problem with the phrase *Google it*.

Google is an Internet search engine tool and the name of a company; in other words, it's not a process by which a person can search the Internet. Besides, is it really that much easier to say *Google it* rather than to say *Do a Google search* or *Search for that on the Internet*?

Wikipedia the word *Google* if you want to learn more.

Headquarters

A *quarter* has many definitions, but in terms of *headquarters*, the meaning of importance is *housing accommodations*. Therefore, *headquarters* is the main accommodation, typically of a business, such as *The headquarters of Acme is in Buffalo.* It is clearly a place, which is a noun.

There is no logical reason to turn an accommodation into a verb, as in *He headquarters in Buffalo* unless it also makes sense to say that *He buildings in Buffalo* or *I university at Harvard.*

Leverage

One of the disadvantages of a language in which nouns are turned into verbs for mere convenience or in order to try to sound more intelligent is that it's difficult for people to know which nouns can be appropriately used as verbs. *Leverage* is one of those words; it's definitely a noun, as in *I'm going to use my position in the company as leverage to get the job done.* What's much less clear is whether using it as a verb is correct. It's listed in most dictionaries as a verb, but dictionaries, as I mentioned in the introduction, are more of a collection of current language than a collection of correct grammar.

I'm going to *leverage* my position as the author of this book to urge restricting its use to the noun form.

Limousine

Limousine? That's right—some people have actually taken to calling this luxurious way to travel as the traveling process itself, as in *I limousined to my publisher in New York.* This is another entry that's more of a word of warning than it is a concern that everyone is going to *limousine* here and *limousine* there, and the concern is that we're only one step away from *planing* across the country or *training* to our vacation spot or *subwaying* into work.

Meeting

A *meeting* is both a noun and a verb. As a noun, it is the actual group of people getting together for a shared purpose, as in *We have a 10 a.m. meeting in the conference room*. As a verb, it is the process of getting together, as in *I'm meeting with the group in the conference room* or *I'm going to meet with him for the second time this week*.

Meeting should not, however, be used as a verb to mean the process of having a meeting, as in *I meetinged with the office staff this morning*. We certainly don't need to invent a word for that; we already have *met*, as in *I met with the office staff this morning* or *I will meet with the office staff this morning*.

Anyone who even thinks about using the new non-word needs fewer meetings and more grammar tutors.

Mentor

A *mentor* is a counselor, guide, or role model, often for a younger person. While a *mentor* might take a great deal of action in that role, a *mentor* is a person and not an action. In other words, a person is a *mentor*; he or she does not do *mentoring*.

Take being a mentor seriously; part of your responsibilities should include being a great role model in how you speak.

Message

Using the word *message* as a verb, such as *We have to be careful how we message this*, is a good example of sounding less than intelligent when the process of turning a noun into a verb first begins. In fact, it makes as much sense as saying *We have to be careful how we paper this* since messages are often written on paper.

I assume that using *message* as a verb sounds as strange to most people as it does to me, but if the trend continues, then many of us will get used to it or assume that it's right and start to mimic it, thereby perpetuating the error.

Office

An office is a place of business (*The office is on Third Avenue*), or it can be the group of professionals who are part of a business (*The entire office attended Joe's retirement party*). Some religious sects consider an office to be a particular service, and our neighbors across the Atlantic (the British) consider the office the part of the house where servants do their work. You'll notice that all of these definitions are places or things; they're not actions. In other words, trying to turn the word *office* into an action, such as *I office on Third Avenue* is incorrect.

Maybe there's so little going on in the *office* that we'll try anything to make us look busy!

Parent

Many children don't think that their *parents* do enough, but it seems a bit drastic to actually turn a *parent* into a verb as punishment.

This noun-to-verb transformation has been accepted by many, so it should be used at your own discretion, but my *parents* have done enough already.

Partner

A *partner* can be a spouse, confidante, business associate, or even a dancer, and although it has become acceptable to use it as a verb, as in *We're going to partner with Acme Corporation to maximize our profits*, it is not acceptable to all.

Let's think back to the best-known dancing duo in history, Ginger Rogers and Fred Astaire. Does it sound more correct to say that *Fred Astaire partnered with Ginger Rogers* or that *Fred Astaire and Ginger Rogers were partners*? The latter sounds more natural since that's the way we've been using the word for generations. The verb usage of the word is a recent development and still not completely accepted, so it's best to avoid it.

Party

We all know that a *party* is something that we go to, and whether we're celebrating a birthday, anniversary, or housewarming, it typically lasts for a few hours. Using *party* as a verb has become popular in the past couple of decades, and people who use it are usually referring to different kinds of parties. These *parties* usually last for a couple of days or occur four times a week, as in *Dude, I partied all weekend* or *I party all the time*.

Using *party* as a verb is not only grammatically incorrect but might not represent a lifestyle that will make your parents proud.

Plate

There are a couple of instances when the word *plate* can be correctly used as a verb, most notably when talking about coating something with a metal (*The inexpensive jewelry was plated with silver*); however, unless you serve metal-coated food, then it should never be used to describe the process of putting food on a plate (*I'll plate the food*). This trend seems to have started as more and more celebrity chefs appeared on television, bringing this grammatically incorrect word to the table, so to speak.

Think of it this way: If a person can *plate food*, then logically, he can also *glass water*. Try saying *Will you glass me some water?* the next time you're thirsty.

Referenced

Using *reference* as a verb, as in *I referenced the information in my report*, has become very popular over the past couple of years even though the usage of *reference* as a verb had fallen out of favor since it was created, which was at the very end of the nineteenth century.

In other words, those who fall into the trap of using nouns as verbs might have lucked out on this one. It's still preferable, though, to say *I made a reference to the information in my report* if you're concerned about sounding too trendy.

Re-purpose

A *purpose* is a reason, not an action. For example, *The purpose of this book is to improve communication* means *The reason for this book is to improve communication*. There is no logical reason for the word *re-purpose* unless you can have a *re-reason*, and even if there were such a thing as a *re-reason*, then it would still be a noun.

That is why the trend of using *re-purpose* as a verb, as in *I'm going to re-purpose this bookshelf as an entertainment center*, cannot possibly be correct; and it will lead to the trend of using *purpose* as a verb, which will also be incorrect.

You don't have to *use* something for a different purpose in order to *use* it again, so there's nothing wrong with the old, reliable word *reuse*, as in *I'm going to reuse the bookshelf as an entertainment center*. Either that or buy a new entertainment center.

Retail

If I'm given a choice between *retail* and *wholesale*, then I'll take wholesale every time. Also, if I'm given the choice between saying *I'm going to retail this product* or *I'm going to wholesale it*, then I'm going to shop somewhere else—most likely a place that keeps nouns as nouns!

Scrapbooking

We all need a good hobby, and putting all of our memorabilia into an organized collection (creating a *scrapbook*) is a reasonable choice. It also gives us an opportunity to take part in that national hobby of turning nouns into verbs since it's now become customary to refer to the process of *making a scrapbook* as the non-word *scrapbooking*.

I doubt that there are many philatelists (stamp collectors) who refer to the process of collecting stamps as *philatelisting*.

Tasked

Tasked, again, will appear in many dictionaries as a verb; however, using the word for a shortened way of assigning someone a task, as in *I tasked him with finishing the report by Monday,* is most certainly a trendy twenty-first-century invention.

All of these *tasks* might get done much more quickly if we didn't assign a noun to try to do a verb's job.

Transition

A *transition* is the change from one form to another. It's not the act of changing, but it's the change itself. For example, *The word transition has undergone the transition from a noun to a verb over the past couple of years* is correct. It is not correct to say that *The word transition has transitioned from a noun to a verb over the past couple of years.*

4

Abused and Misused
CONTRIVED WORDS AND WORDS
USED INCORRECTLY

We're human, which means that we have a tendency to want to sound the same as everyone else, or we sometimes try to prove how smart we are with the words we choose. These are two of the more common reasons for using legitimate words incorrectly or for using fabricated non-words when established, current words would work as well as they have for the past century or two.

Humans also want to be correct, right? That's why we should put all of those new non-words and misused words into a giant green bag, take it to the curb, and stand there until the bag is tossed into the back of the garbage truck. I fully support recycling plastic and glass—but not these words.

Actionable

Actionable has to do with whether there are grounds for a lawsuit or for court proceedings, which might have been an appropriate word to use around the shredder during the last days of Enron. In most companies, though, words such as *lawsuits* and *court proceedings* make people a little nervous. All other uses of the word are grammatically incorrect, for example, using *actionable* as a way to ask whether an action should be taken on something.

Big-Time

I might have more to say about using *big-time*—or more accurately about not using it—if I had any idea of how or why it's used. *Big-time* seems to be sometimes used as a complex adverb, if there is such a thing, as if it were an acceptable substitution for the word *very*, which *is* also an adverb. However, it's usually put at the end of a sentence, as in *I'm excited big-time*, rather than immediately ahead of the word it's modifying as is typical with *very*, as in *I'm very excited*. My suspicion is that *big-time* is put at the end for emphasis, but putting slang at the end of a sentence just emphasizes slang.

An older, more established use of the word is as a noun. It might have been popular in the 1930s to say that *I can't wait until I hit the big time* as a reference to striking it rich or becoming successful. It's rarely used that way now, but it's still just slang, and using slang in any situation or from any generation makes the speaker sound less than articulate.

Biweekly

Biweekly has always meant, and will always mean, *every other week*. A couple of decades after lower verbal SAT standards at business colleges, though, and we now have a work world half filled with people who think it means twice a week and half filled with people who get it right. The confusion has resulted in many missed meetings, which, depending on a person's perspective, might not be a bad thing.

Make it easy by saying what is intended, whether it's every other week or twice a week. The same goes for *bimonthly*.

Charged

You can be *charged* with burglary; you can *take charge* of a situation; you can *charge* an enemy; the air can be *charged* with electricity or energy; you can even *charge* for a service performed. There may even be a few other acceptable ways in which the word *charge* may be used as a verb, including giving forceful or authoritative instruction (*the inspector was charged with finding the murderer*); however, although some may disagree, *charge* should not be used for assigning menial, everyday tasks, as in *The staff assistant was charged with ordering the bagels for the meeting* since ordering bagels isn't typically considered something that requires much force or authority.

Cheesy

Not being a fan of slang, it's tough for me to say what *cheesy* actually means. It seems to be used as an adjective that describes something done without class or sophistication or some event that was done in an inexpensive or insincere way. For example, a *cheesy* wedding might be one held at the local fire hall with the chicken dance as the bridal dance. A ceremony at city hall where the mayor's biggest contributor is given the key to the city might be viewed as *cheesy*.

Being more of a fan of food than slang, though, I know that *cheesy* nachos are the ones I prefer, and I will limit my use of *cheesy* to references involving food.

Conversate

When the accent is on the second syllable, *converse* means to have a discussion with others, such as *I'm going to converse with my boss about getting a raise. Conversate* is a newly invented word that means to have a discussion with others.

When you notice two nearly identical words that mean the same thing, and one has been around for generations while the other was invented last week, it's safe to say that the most recent one isn't really a word.

Please don't *conversate* with anyone.

Craveable

Craveable was born in the world of fast-food advertising, but it seems to be destined to be served up in all types of informal conversation. The apparent definition is *appetizing*, as in *The chili fries were craveable*; however, the best way to describe real food is with real words, of which *craveable* is not one.

Curiouser

The use of the non-word *curiouser*, which is most commonly misused in duplicate in the phrase *curiouser and curiouser*, is proof that people tend to repeat what they've heard so quickly that they don't stop to consider whether what they're saying is correct.

In order to believe that *curiouser* would be correct, we would need to believe that *curiousest* is also correct. The error could spread to that, but it might not happen any time soon since that would be quite a tongue twister.

Disaccumulate

Disaccumulate has recently started to appear in the English language as a way of expressing the opposite of *accumulate*, such as *He started to disaccumulate wealth when the stock market fell*. It's not a word, and as a former meteorologist, I hate to think that weather forecasters are soon going to have to start forecasting *snow disaccumulations*; we've always had enough trouble forecasting how much is going to fall.

Empower

Oprah has done great things in her life and with her show; however, I blame her for the misuse of the word *empower*. During every show, invariably, one of her guests, a member of the audience, or even Oprah, herself, talks about feeling *empowered*.

Empower means to give official authority or legal power to. People already have official authority and legal power over themselves. People say *empower* to mean that they feel powerful, in control of their lives, or both.

So that's what they should start saying.

Freaking

Freaking is a slang non-word that we substitute for the actual curse that's intended, and that should be reason enough to avoid it. Besides, while it might be less offensive to those listening, we're not fooling anyone; the intention is the same, and it's not as if the word were an otherwise stellar addition to the collective vocabulary.

Darn it. Why do we do things like that?

Freakin' Me Out

Speaking of *freaking* annoying phrases . . .

Should *It's freakin' me out* and *I'm freakin' out* and *I'm freaked out* no longer be said because the only logical assumption is that stupid sentences would be used only by stupid people? Should they be banned from the English language because they're yet another fine example of slang that has started to spread into the mainstream culture? Should we stop saying them because they're used in nearly every conversation, which renders them ineffective? Or should we stop these ridiculous things because it makes no sense to use the word *freaking* as a verb?

Pick one of those or find another reason—it doesn't matter. Just find a reason, and stop saying it.

Functional

Functional means that something works, meaning it performs a function—nothing more, nothing less. The sofa is *functional* if you can sit on it, and the kitchen is *functional* if all the plumbing and appliances work properly and it has storage space. Because of the home-renovation craze of the past several years, it has become acceptable to say that something is not *functional* if it doesn't look the way we want it to look or work in the way we want it to work.

For instance, many people now say that the sofa is no longer *functional* because the color or style is outdated. That's incorrect. It's no longer *functional* if it has a broken leg or no cushions. It's not any less *functional* because it's covered in peach flowers; it's simply out of style. If everything in the kitchen works, but you want more cupboard space, room for the George Foreman Grill, and stainless-steel appliances, then say that the kitchen needs to be more modern or redesigned.

We shouldn't change the meaning of a word so that the word conforms to what might be convenient; we should alter our word choices to say what we mean while conforming to existing, standard definitions.

Ginormous

I think we all know *ginormous* is a combination of *gigantic* and *enormous*, which is another way of saying that it's not a word.

Impactful

It's too pedestrian for some of us to use a phrase such as *It will have a great impact* when we could use *impactful*, thinking it sounds more intelligent. That might be true if *impactful* were actually a word.

Ka-Ching

Is it *ka-ching* or is it *ca-ching* or *cha-ching*? It's hard to say since it's not a word, which should be enough of a reason to stop making a sound that resembles someone trying to rid himself of phlegm.

If that's not reason enough, then stop saying that non-word because it's completely devoid of any style, grace, or intelligence. Saying *ka-ching* when someone mentions money is as tasteful as licking your lips whenever food is mentioned.

No-Brainer

The "word" *no-brainer* makes no sense, unless something that requires thinking can be considered a *brainer*; it's pure slang. And the overuse of *no-brainer* has promoted it from informal usage into use in our daily and even professional lives. Can we start underusing it to the point that it will disappear before it ends up like *ain't*, which has started to appear in dictionaries as colloquial instead of what it used to be, which was substandard?

Okayed/OK'd

It pains me to even type the "word" *okayed*, as in *The boss okayed (OK'd) the budget.*

OK and *okay* are, at best, slang adjectives, which means that they should be used only in the most informal of settings, such as saying it to a friend at the barbecue pit when planning to use the services of a designated driver. But to try to turn the non-word adjective into a non-word verb and use it in more formal situations, such as in front of the person who decides if you're bright enough to get that promotion, is, well, less than *OK*.

Phraseology

The suffix *-ology* generally means *the study of. Psychology*, for example, means *the study of the mind* (psyche). *Sociology*, of course, means *the study of society. Biology* is *the study of life* (bios). *Meteorology* means *the study of meteors*—wait, that's not right. It means *the study of the atmosphere.* (It's not as wrong as it might seem, though, since our ancestors assumed that the weather had to do with the stars, thus the name.)

Logically, then, *phraseology* would mean *the study of phrases* or something similar; however, *phraseology* seems to mean the manner in which thoughts are expressed, as in *The phraseology in the report is too technical for the average reader.*

That doesn't make sense unless you're of the opinion that contrived words can mean whatever we'd like them to mean; then *phraseology* could mean the *manner in which thoughts are expressed*—or it could mean *the study of green bananas.* Maybe we could find a different word to replace phraseology; how about *The language in the report is too technical for the average reader?*

Physicality/Commonality

The same person who says *impactful* (see earlier in this chapter) probably also says *commonality* and *physicality*. The same mindset of thinking that one larger word is more effective than a couple of words is at work here. That's the reason for saying that *The physicality of the defense was impressive* rather than *The physical style of the defense was impressive* or *The commonality of the two products was obvious* rather than *The common attributes of the two products were obvious*.

Unfortunately, the logicality fails when we don't use real words.

Plagued

Plagued is another debatable entry. Some people, such as I, believe that the proper use of the word *plague*, whether as a noun or a verb, has to make some reference to deadly disease or some other type of pestilence. Others believe that *plague* can be used as a synonym for *bother* or *annoy*, such as *Jimmy's father plagued him about doing his homework*.

Well, maybe if Jimmy were studying entomology, I could make an exception.

Proactive

My disdain for the "word" *proactive* is so extreme (since I didn't think it was a word) that I decided I needed to take action before I harmed the next person who uttered the word in my presence; in other words, most people would say I was taking a *proactive* approach. Dust was flying as I tossed books aside while looking for my oldest, most trusted dictionary—circa 1954. I needed to confirm that it, indeed, wasn't a word so that I could urge its banishment.

That dictionary confirmed my suspicions that it was not a word, at least in its mainstream sense; however, I was surprised to learn that it was, in fact, a word dating back to the 1930s. At that time, it was a technical word used in the discipline in psychology.

The new usage of *proactive* is supposed to be the opposite of *reactive*. The problem, of course, is that *proactive* already means something else. In other words, in its new incarnation, *proactive* is one of those catchy non-words that has taken on a life of its own (now there's a good trendy phrase) and, according to most people, has become a word. Perhaps that's all we need in order to have a new word—just start saying something often enough so that everyone thinks it's a word, and then it is.

All I know is that we used to have other ways of saying that we need to act now in order to prevent a future problem, including, well, *Take action before it becomes a problem* or the words *anticipate*, *intervene*, and *prevent*. I also know that the "word" *proactive* is now more popular than a pair of blue suede shoes at a Memphis auction, which means that it's not an effective way to communicate.

Verticality/Verticalness

Vertical means *perpendicular to the horizon*. There are not degrees of *vertical*; something is either perpendicular to the horizon or it's not, which means that there is no degree of *verticalness* or no *verticality*. These are invented words.

Is it just a matter of time until we start to hear *horizontality* or *horizontalness* or *perpendicularness*?

Who'd've Thunk It

Another bit of popular non-word slang is *Who'd've thunk it*. If you can't spell it, then don't say it, especially when it sounds that stupid.

5

That Makes No Sense, Captain Kirk
ILLOGICAL WORDS
AND PHRASES

Many words, phrases, and expressions in our language simply make no sense. Either the phrase has lost what was once a legitimate reason for its existence or it is, as Spock would say to Captain Kirk, completely illogical.

If we would ever slow down long enough to think about what we were saying rather than spewing out the first prepared catchphrase that comes to mind, then we might avoid many of these problems rather than moving at a Mach 7 speed toward a language black hole. Or as Scotty might say, *The engine's gonna blow, Captain!*

Called on the Carpet

While I know that to be *called on the carpet* means to be *reprimanded in a harsh way*, I had no idea why this phrase was used until I did some research. *Carpet* is an old British word that means *reprimand*.

I'm sure that I'm not the only one who thought the phrase had something to do with a floor covering, so those who still think it does will need to update their vocabulary to include the phrase *called on the laminate hardwood* since that's a little more in style.

Centers Around

An *oxymoron* is a figure of speech that is contradictory, such as *artificial intelligence*, and *centers around* is an example of a widely used oxymoron. A *center* is the middle point, and *around* means *in a circle* or *surrounding*; therefore, if you *center around* something, you will never get there.

Use *centers on* instead.

Coeds

Coed is a term used for a female student at a learning institution where both male and female students are permitted to attend, which used to be called a coeducational facility. Assigning the term to refer to just the female student doesn't make sense since the coeducation facility clearly accepts both male and female students; not only could the male student just as easily be considered a *coed*, but he is, in fact, also a *coed*.

The term must have sexist roots. Since it was the female who changed the university from an educational facility to a coeducational facility, the female students were assigned the new term. We've tried to exclude other sexist terms from the language, and *coed* can join that list.

Epic Proportion/Biblical Proportion

The word *proportion* should always be used as a comparative relationship between two or more things, such as *Since I gained weight, my stomach is out of proportion to the rest of my body.*

In other words, to properly use the word *proportion*, we must always relate one thing to something else. That's why *epic* and *biblical* are so often attached to the word *proportion*—they're a way of saying that the event is comparable to a great event of the past. However, by its definition—comparing it to an event of biblical times or of epic size—means that these phrases should rarely be used since events of that nature generally don't occur during an individual's lifetime.

They're now commonly misused just to say that something is *big*, such as *Last week's storm was of biblical proportion*. Chances are that the person is just trying to say that the storm was *big* rather than comparing the storm to the one that brought rain for forty days and forty nights.

Foreseeable Future

Alliteration is as much fun as a french fry festival in Fredericksburg, but sometimes a phonetically friendly phrase, such as *foreseeable future*, is more frilly than factual.

It's understood that the short-term future, such as what hotel you'll be staying at after you've planned your vacation or what time you'll be having dinner tonight, might be projected with enough accuracy to ignore the fact that seeing into the future— any future—is literally impossible, but unless you want to re-live the glory days of the Psychic Hotline, we should stop using this generally illogical phrase so indiscriminately.

Go Figure

I know that by now you're probably thinking, "Gee, this guy thinks he knows everything about everything," but this one has me stumped. I simply don't get it. What does the expression *go figure* mean? It's used as a sarcastic expression of surprise—*that* I understand. For example, a statement such as *I hear that the price of gas has gone up again, and Exxon has reported record profits* might elicit a *go figure* in response, but what does it mean?

Maybe it means that it doesn't take much analysis to reach that conclusion, but I've never *gone and figured* anything, so I'm a bit at a loss.

Help the Problem

We say *That's not going to help the problem* as if we actually wanted the *problem* to become worse; we want to *help* it. We want *the problem* to become bigger, stronger, and faster than it used to be. Perhaps we're trying to make it into the $6,000,000 problem.

The solution is what needs some help, meaning we want to *solve the problem*.

I Could Be Wrong, But/If I Had to Guess

The phrases *I could be wrong, but* and *if I had to guess* have never been made by anyone who actually thought she was wrong or thought she was guessing. Why the false modesty?

I Could Care Less

Great mysteries abound. Who built the pyramids in Egypt? Is there life after death? Who invented the word *infomercial*? But one of the greatest mysteries of all is why so many people get the phrase *I couldn't care less* wrong.

Let's just say that you're a vegetarian who has never been to Philadelphia. A friend reports that a sandwich shop opened in town that specializes in Philadelphia-style cheesesteaks. If you wanted to effectively communicate that the new restaurant is of no interest to you, then which of the following phrases would be more appropriate: *I couldn't care less* or *I could care less*?

I could care less says that you could actually care less than you already do, implying that you might have some degree of concern. The correct answer is *I couldn't care less* if, in fact, there is no way that you could possibly care less than you do.

I could care less might be a mistaken version of the sarcastic and similar response *I could almost care* and the correct phrase *I couldn't care less*, but you may as well get it right—not that I care.

I Just Want to Give You a Heads-Up

When someone yelled *Heads up!* when I was playing ball in the streets of my youth in order to alert me to look up to find the ball or to alert me to a base runner approaching from behind, I usually ducked, which seems to be the opposite of what I was instructed to do. Now, several decades later, when I hear *I just wanted to give you a heads-up* from someone who wants to inform me of something that I need to know—either at work or at home or with friends or with people I just met—I either cringe or slowly back out of the room.

Back then, it was because I wasn't much of a baseball player; now, it's because I'm not much for hearing the same, overly informal phrase day after day after day.

I'm Not One to Complain, But/Not to Belabor the Point, But

Never once in the history of the English language has the phrase *I'm not one to complain, but* not been followed by a complaint. Similarly, never once has the phrase *not to belabor the point, but* not been followed by further discussion.

I'm not one to tell people what not to do, but we should stop prefacing a statement by stating that we're not going do exactly what we are about to do.

I'm So Mad I Could Spit

If you're truly so angry that you want to gather some saliva in your mouth and let it fly, then you must be as angry as you ever get, which, unless anger management is a problem, should be rare. In those few situations, don't use a phrase that everyone else uses; invent a new phrase, such as *I'm so angry I want to put on my golf shoes and toss the five-iron into the water hazard by the fourteenth hole.*

It Goes Without Saying, But

Is there anyone out there who doesn't know why we shouldn't say *It goes without saying, but*?

It should, in fact, *go without saying*, **but** since people keep saying it, it must not be true. Saying *it goes without saying* right before you say something is analogous to saying *I'm not going to the store, and while I'm there, would you like me to pick up something for you?*

It's Not Over Until the Fat Lady Sings

It's not over until the fat lady sings doesn't make much sense. While I understand that the *fat lady* being referred to is an opera star, since this fat lady sings at the beginning, middle, and end of most operas, why would *it*, whatever *it* is, be *over* whenever *she sings*? In most instances, *it* would be over before *it* gets very far!

Perhaps it's a reference to the fact that many operas have a closing scene in which the opera star sings an emotional solo, but if that's the reason that this phrase has lived in infamy for lo these many decades, then it's time to close the curtains on this long-running, overdone show.

It's to Die For

I love cheesecake as much as anyone, but I've never seriously considered trading a slice of the creamy delight for my life. I know. I know. People don't *literally* (see Chapter 1) mean that they'd die for the piece of cheesecake; it's an expression—although with the fat and cholesterol in cheesecake, it might be close to being literal. Anyway, if you're using exaggeration for effect, then it would be much more effective to use an expression that doesn't bore us all.

No, Thank *You*

Common courtesy requires that the correct response to *Thank you* is *You're welcome*; however, it has become more and more common in recent years for a *Thank you* to be followed by a *No, thank you* or just *Thank you*.

This undoubtedly started when a mutual service was being provided. For example, a clerk at a store might thank a customer for his patronage, and the customer, in turn, might thank the clerk for the personal service. There is a better way. The customer should respond with *You're welcome* after being thanked and then thank the clerk before leaving.

Unless you're practicing to win the Miss Congeniality title, a simple *You're welcome* will suffice.

Reinvent Yourself

People who have become *empowered* (see Chapter 4) often decide it's time to *reinvent themselves*. That's incorrect—twice.

Only an inventor could possibly *reinvent* anything. That leaves the rest of us completely out of the reinventing-of-themselves business. If you are a clone of yourself that you created in your own basement, then I could give you partial credit. There's still a catch, however; even if you invented something, it can't be *reinvented*. It may have taken Thomas Edison longer than he might have liked to *invent* that first working light bulb, but he'd still be trying to *invent* the next first working light bulb.

Sure Bet

Many a gambler has lost his proverbial shirt on a *sure bet*. A *bet* is, of course, a risk; adding the word *sure*, which removes uncertainty, doesn't make any sense or make the outcome any more certain.

That's Nothing to Sneeze At

While I certainly don't understand the logic, it's apparent that the phrase *That's nothing to sneeze at* seems to mean we shouldn't sneeze at things that are worthwhile. Logically, then, if there are things that are not worth sneezing at, there must be things that *are* worth sneezing at—that is, things that aren't worthwhile.

Until people start confusing allergy season with the season of discontent, though, I'm going to have to recommend that we do away with this ridiculous phrase.

Tons More

We've all undoubtedly heard that a *ton of feathers weighs as much as a ton of lead*. That's certainly true since both weigh 2,000 pounds; it just takes a much larger quantity of feathers than it does lead to make a ton.

My question, for the ton-obsessed among us, is how much time, space, or fun is required to make a *ton* or even several *tons*? *I'm going to have tons more time when summer vacation starts* or *We had tons of fun at the amusement park* or *I'm going to have tons more space when I move* are all examples of things that don't weigh 2,000 pounds.

If you can't weigh it, then you can't have *tons* of it.

Wrong-Headed Thinking

While *forward thinking* (see Chapter 6) may indeed be inarticulate and trendy, it certainly makes more sense than *wrong-headed thinking* since I'm not even sure of what it means, which I'm guessing means that others are confused as well. Does *wrong-headed thinking* mean *erroneous thinking*—that the thought process itself was erroneous? Or does it mean the action taken was incorrect—that the result of the thinking was wrong?

I recommend *right-headed thinking*, which means replacing the phrase with something that will be easy for the listener to understand.

6

It's All Bad . . . Believe Me
EXCESSIVELY TRENDY WORDS
AND EXPRESSIONS

A *trend* is something that by definition is just not good enough to become a permanent part of the culture. It comes in like a thundercloud, and before you know it, it's gone more quickly than an April snow.

The argument can be made that being trendy while the trend is popular is more than acceptable—it's actually desirable. Sure, it's important to know what's going on in the world, but there's a difference between responding to legitimate changes in society and jumping on every pop-culture bandwagon that rolls down the highway. In the 1990s, it was wise for people in business to know about the Internet and understand its potential implications; in the 1980s, it was not as wise for a woman to stock up on stirrup pants in every imaginable color of the rainbow because she thought they were going to be a wardrobe staple for decades to come.

More important, though, is that sounding intelligent is preferable to sounding stylish, especially since sounding intelligent is never a passing trend. Many current word trends are grammatically incorrect, and that alone should keep us from *trendizing*. See, I can invent trendy words, too.

24/7

Using the numbers 24/7 as a shortcut for words in order to express that someone or something is always available or open is done mainly out of laziness or a desire to be trendy. Besides, other than as a reference to grocery stores or all-night pharmacies, the sentiment is usually not accurate. If someone says that he's working on a project or is available for questions 24/7, then call him at 4:30 a.m. to test his sincerity.

At the End of the Day

Speaking of the *end of the day*, I'd like to make it to the *end of a day*—any day—without hearing the phrase *at the end of the day* multiple times. Of course, given the number of times that this phrase is used, that would probably mean that I'd have to remain home alone for the entire day without talking to anyone, checking my e-mail, reading anything on the Internet, or turning on the television.

Not only is the phrase hopelessly overused, which makes it

ineffective, but it's often used instead of a more articulate phrase. For instance, *When the project is completed, we'll have a stronger product line* is more precise than *At the end of the day, we'll have a stronger product line.*

In other words, *At the end of the day, I'd rather speak in concrete terms rather than amorphous clichés.*

Brainstorm

Is *brainstorm* an adjective, as in *a brainstorming session*? Is it a verb, as in *We brainstormed on the new project this morning*? Is it a noun, as in *I just had a brainstorm*? Or is it just another trendy non-word that has quickly been added to our collective vocabulary?

All I know is that I would like to informally get a group of people together in order to try to find alternatives to using the word *brainstorming.*

Challenges

My frustration about soft-selling *problems* will become even more clear when I discuss *issues* later in this chapter; however, saying *challenges* is certainly another back-handed way of talking about problems. It used to be that only the most problem-phobic among us would say something similar to *I'm having challenges with this project* when what was meant was *I'm having problems with this project*. Most of us would reserve the use of the word *challenge* to describe a call to engage in a contest, as in *Running up that hill was quite a challenge.*

Now, though, we're not permitted to talk about having *a*

difficult time or a *problem* with anyone or anything. I always thought nirvana would be less *challenging*.

Clean Lines/Spa-Like Feel/Dream House

In the world of home decorating and renovating, trends include chocolate brown with blue, granite countertops, stainless-steel appliances, and using the same words over and over again.

Everyone wants to have *clean lines*, as if dirty lines used to be all the rage. Try talking about *straight lines* or *simple lines that give an elegant look*. And as soon as everyone in the country gets his or her wish of creating a *spa-like feel* or *retreat* in the master bedroom and master bath, then the spa industry and hotel business will be doomed.

Finally, too much emphasis on having a *dream house* may not be wise. It becomes so important to some people to try to get that perfect home that the result is an unaffordable mortgage, along with stress-related health problems, and it makes some with modest homes feel inferior to others.

Cool/That's So Cool

Can you believe that the word *cool* is still trendy?

If I'd have written this book in the 1970s, then *cool* would have belonged in the trendy chapter. The same could be said of the 1980s and the 1990s. Is it possible that it's trendy again in the 2000s?

Technically, that's too long to be a trend, but it's my book, and I'm going to keep calling it trendy. I could have put *cool* in any number of places. *Cool* could certainly be in Chapter 9, "That's

Not What I Meant," since it has never expressed an actual thought. Sadly, *cool* could now even be added to Chapter 7, "What a Way to Make a Living," since its use is widespread in the professional world. Also, *cool* doesn't even make any sense unless it refers to temperature, so it could have a fitting home in Chapter 5, "That Makes No Sense, Captain Kirk." I could go on, but I'm so tired of the word that I don't even want to type it again.

For the record, adding the word *dude* after it doesn't help.

Disingenuous and Deliberately Mislead

During the 2004 presidential election, politicians loved to use the word *disingenuous* and the phrase *deliberately mislead*. How many times did John Kerry want to say that President Bush lied about one thing or another but chose instead to say that the president *deliberately misled* us or was *disingenuous*?

Politicians will always be politicians, but that doesn't mean we have to impersonate them. We're adults who can deal with the truth.

The fact is, people lie. The *concern* (see "Issues," later in this chapter)—I mean *problem*—is that we're too nice to say so.

Ever

I already talked about the redundancy of *ever* in *best ever* in Chapter 2; however, the problem with the word extends beyond mere redundancy into the trend toward the need for melodrama in our society. The word *ever* seems to be tossed onto the end of every other sentence in daily conversation, on television, and in advertising.

If it wasn't *the worst day—ever*, then it was *the best pizza—ever*. If it wasn't *the slowest game—ever*, then it was *the greatest catch—ever*. If it wasn't *the biggest sale—ever*, then it was *the longest movie—ever*.

Almost every time that *ever* is added to the end of a thought, it's for the purpose of trying to add emphasis. We don't feel as if it were descriptive enough to just say *I had a bad day*; it would have to be *I had the worst day—ever* in order to grab attention. It has to be dramatic in order to count. The irony is that the overuse actually renders the phrase less effective, negating the intended emphasis.

In addition, the grammatical error of using *ever* at the end of the sentence for the purpose of emphasis or exaggeration could easily be corrected by understanding that its use in this way is merely a shortcut. For example, it would be grammatically correct to say that *Today was the worst day I've ever had* rather than *Today was the worst day—ever*. That would not, however, solve the problem related to melodrama.

Facilitate/Facilitated

I suspected that *facilitate/facilitated* would fall into the same category as *proactive* (see Chapter 4), meaning that I had the right to my nearly equal level of disdain when hearing it. Technically, though, this verb was a word back in the 1950s, but it could be used only when something was made easy or when something reduced the labor of something. People are now using it to mean *get something done*, such as *Can you facilitate the mailing?*

Based on the fact that everyone is *facilitating* one thing or another, it's clear that we don't use it only in its original manner today; otherwise, everything would be going much more smoothly.

Forward Thinking

Saying *forward thinking* might be a natural progression of the trend of saying *going forward* (see Chapter 7) or *as we move forward* rather than using the word *future* or the phrase *in the future*. That would be enough of a reason to stop saying it since it's an unnecessary phrase.

The other possible explanation for *forward thinking* is that we're becoming less articulate since we already have perfectly fine ways of saying that an idea is *innovative* or *creative* or *inventive* or *clever* or *ingenious*. The only difference is that those words say it better.

Friendly

We've become a very *friendly* society! Or maybe we haven't, but we've certainly become a society that likes to stick a *-friendly* on the ends of words rather than just saying what we mean.

User-friendly means that it's *easy for a person to use*, as in *user-friendly instructions*. *Child-friendly*, on the other hand, doesn't usually mean that it's easy for a child to use but, rather, that *something or somewhere is safe enough for children*, as in a *child-friendly neighborhood*. I doubt that *computer-friendly* means that it's easy for the computer to use; it seems to mean that *the computer is easy for a person to use*. (I wonder what a *child-friendly computer* would mean—would it be safe for the child to be around or easy for the child to use?) *Carb-friendly* doesn't have anything to do with people using carbs—which, by the way, isn't even a word—it's *carbohydrates*. *Carb-friendly* means that *a food has a level of carbohydrates that can be beneficial to someone on a low-carbohydrate diet*.

We have four similarly constructed words with four completely different meanings—not exactly *English-friendly*.

Ground Zero

Ground zero was a phrase that originated as a reference for the point of impact for a nuclear bomb—the center of the bomb where all life would be obliterated. It's an awful phrase used to describe a horrific event, and after the use of nuclear bombs to end World War II, the phrase should never have been used again out of respect for the gravity of the event.

The word became popular after the terrorist attacks in September 2001, when reporters tried to describe the horrors of the attack. Now, it's common to use *ground zero* as a reference to any number of things, from the center of a hurricane to the location of a problem on any scale.

The use of the phrase is now disrespectful for two reasons.

Issue

The word *issue* has always meant *topic*, such as *The following issues will be discussed at the company meeting: how many extra vacation days will be given to each employee, whether lunch should be extended to an hour and a half, and when we should start having four-day work weeks*. As you can see, those wouldn't be *problems* for most of us; they'd be *topics* that we'd be happy to discuss.

Somewhere along the line, though, the word *issue* has somehow become synonymous with the word *problem*, such as saying *There's an issue with the copier* when flames are shooting out of the back of the machine or *I have issues with this report* when, in fact, you don't agree with one word in it.

It's hard to know why this transformation has been allowed to take place, but it's probably either because we focus on *problems* so much that we assume every *topic* is viewed as a *problem* or, more likely, we're trying to talk about *problems* in a kind, gentle manner so that others aren't offended. The *issue*—I mean *problem*—with that is twofold. First, everyone now knows that you're talking about a problem when you say *issue*, so it's not working. Second, it leads to confusion among those who prefer to keep using the words in the manner in which they were intended.

Put simply, do not use *issue* as a synonym for *problem*, and, by the way, don't be tempted to use *concern* or *concerns* as an alternative way to say that something is a *problem* when you're afraid to say so. It's not an improvement and leads to the same confusion.

It Is What It Is

For some reason, the phrase *It is what it is* is spreading through the language more quickly than a fire through a match factory. This wasn't even clever the first time; in fact, it doesn't say anything. *It is what it is?* Of course, *it is what it is.* What else could it be?! *It is what it isn't?*

The expression—or should I say instant cliché—seems to be used in several equally inarticulate ways, including the *I don't like it the way it is, but I can't do anything about it anyway* way.

It is sometimes used as a way to deflect responsibility. For example, when a professional football player drops the potential game-winning touchdown in the end zone with one second left in the game, he might say in the press conference *It is what it is* rather than *I'm the reason that we're not going to the Super Bowl. Sorry about that.*

It is also used as a way to be dismissive, sort of the twenty-first-century version of the 1990s ever-popular response *whatever*. Perhaps Sarah calls Betsy to say that her boyfriend, Billy, has decided to have an operation to become Billie, but Betsy is more interested in watching *American Idol*, so she responds with, *I guess it is what it is. Take care now.*

Copycat versions of *It is what it is*, such as *They are what they are*, *They do what they do*, and *I am what I am*, are not any better. In fact, not only are they inarticulate, but people will conclude that you're still *thinking inside the box* (see "Think Outside the Box," later in this chapter).

It's All Good/My Bad

Every generation invents a series of phrases, words, and expressions; it's a natural process of creating an identity. The current group includes *It's all good*, *My bad*, *back in the day* (see Chapter 13), *bling*, *crib*, and *Show me some love*. Before jumping on the youthful bandwagon, consider the following.

Anyone older than the current generation who uses those

words in an attempt to seem young or trendy is like the forty-five-year-old man who has a ponytail because he thinks long hair will make him look younger. Not only does it not work, but it does the opposite. The forty-five-year-old ends up looking like a fifty-five-year-old who's trying to recapture a distant youth. A hairstyle appropriate for his age will allow him to look like a forty-five-year-old who takes care of himself, which is more consistent with his goal. Similarly, anyone over thirty-five who tries to use the latest trendy catch phrases makes herself sound even older than she is. No one is being fooled.

Besides, all of the new phrases come and go as quickly as fad clothing. In less than a decade, the new, trendy words will be as appropriate as mullets, and people who have become addicted to using them will be out of style.

Kick It Up a Notch/Bam!

Unless you receive a standing ovation when you include "gahlic" (that's *garlic* for those of you who don't speak Emeril-ese) in a recipe or have a live band performing in your kitchen, *Kick it up a notch* and *Bam!* should remain behind the closed pantry doors. You know what I'm talking about.

Low Carb

People want to lose weight, and an excess of carbohydrates in their diet can play a role in being overweight; however, the goal of weight loss is to lose body weight, not language weight. The proper phrase is *low carbohydrate*, not the alphabet-diet-reduced *low carb*.

Just as with good weight-loss plans, good language skills don't involve shortcuts. Don't fall into the language equivalent of the water diet by abbreviating words that might be, well, big boned.

Meltdown

Meltdowns are happening all over the place—at work when a presenter falters, at home when someone has an emotional outburst or breakdown, and on television when a star player has a poor performance in a big game. *Meltdown* has been said so frequently for so many years—and its frequency seems to be increasing—that many of us have probably forgotten the source of the word.

It's actually jargon used to describe a serious accident within a nuclear reactor—an accident in which tens of thousands or even millions of people might be negatively affected or even killed. Perhaps there might be better ways to describe our relatively minor problems.

Multitasking

During the past decade, either the ability of human beings to perform tasks has improved (evolution in action), or we have changed the way we label work. In other words, either people have learned to *multitask*, or we have invented a new word that says nothing. My vote's with the latter.

First of all (as discussed in Chapter 3), *task* is a noun, not a verb. Besides, when we work, we don't literally do multiple tasks at the same time, which is what multitasking is supposed to mean. We don't type a memo while talking to a client and preparing a presentation unless it doesn't matter whether the memo is correct or the client receives decent service. When a boss wants someone to *multitask*, he wants the person to be able to handle a multitude of tasks, and he also wants the worker to be able to switch back and forth quickly from one task to the next in order to be efficient.

Use nouns as nouns, and try to have an understanding that we can do only one task at time—unless walking and gum chewing are considered tasks where you work.

People Gravitate Toward the Kitchen

If we were better hosts, then our guests wouldn't have to sweat while hovering around a hot stove before dinner or linger on uncomfortable dining room chairs after dinner while a soft couch sits only a room away.

People don't *gravitate toward the kitchen* as if there were a magnetic field sucking them in. It's an inaccurate statement that is best avoided; a more accurate statement would be that *people gravitate toward the kitchen because that's where the host is.*

Find a way to serve dinner and properly tend to your guests.

Pushing the Envelope

The manuscript I just sent my publisher was so large that I really had to *push the envelope* to get it to fit. Wait, that's not what the phrase *pushing the envelope* means. It seems to mean that someone is trying to expand the boundaries of what is considered acceptable, whether that be in the entertainment industry or work environment.

Howard Stern is often considered one who *pushes the envelope*. We'd be better off if we said that Howard Stern is attempting to lower the standards of television and radio through the degradation of women. Then people would know what's going on and be able to take a responsible view on the topic.

Think Outside the Box

Has any phrase lost its charm more quickly than *think outside the box*?

The phrase can be effective the first time it's told to a group of people because it might allow someone to consider problems in new ways; however, clever quips work only once. When heard for even the second time, much of their clever qualities have already been lost. Now that *think outside the box* is said more often than *we need to think of a new approach*, the idea behind the phrase has become secondary to jokes about the phrase, such as not remembering being in a box or how certain members of management might belong in a box or . . .

The phrase is now a trite way to try to encourage people to think in a non-trite manner, which is not very effective but *is*, however, ironic.

Threw Him Under the Bus

I'm glad that I'm not a bus driver since so many people are getting *thrown under the bus* that I wouldn't be able to afford liability insurance. Seriously, this has been a mildly annoying phrase for years, but its elevation from occasionally being used in informal situations to always being used in every situation, including at work and in the media, means that it's time to permanently park the phrase in the junkyard.

Visionary

A *visionary* is supposed to be a person with the insight and knowledge to anticipate trends and the needs of society in order to create solutions for future problems. Unfortunately, *visionary*, like many words, has come to be defined almost exclusively on the basis of business success. We are more likely to deem the businessman who is responsible for implementing a more cost-effective way to process oil into gasoline a *visionary* rather than the scientist who painstakingly works on a nonpolluting alternative to fossil fuels for the future.

The scientist is more of a *visionary* by the intended definition of the word; however, the businessman is considered *visionary* because of our new standards. When business defines our words, it also defines our lives. Do we really want people who care only about profits making our most important decisions?

Worst-Case Scenario

The *worst-case scenario* is that we'll continue to use this phrase so often that all of the other ways of discussing *a negative outcome* or *possible negative outcome* will be eliminated from our formerly robust language.

The *best-case scenario* is that we'll start to speak more creatively or at least stop repeating the same prefabricated phrases.

Wrap My Brain Around It

Rather than it being a passing pop-culture fad destined for the scrap heap of language, as was my hope when I first heard it, *wrap my brain around it* seems to be gaining in popularity. I'm not sure why we need another way to say *I don't understand* or *I'm having a difficult time making sense of this* or even *I'm confused*, but, apparently, we do.

If we need something new, then at least invent an expression that doesn't make me think of a 1950s B-movie about a mad professor with a lab full of brains in formaldehyde.

7

What a Way to Make a Living
INEFFECTIVE WORKPLACE WORDS AND EXPRESSIONS

The average person works forty hours per week, which means that approximately one-third of our waking lives is spent at our jobs. Whose idea was that, anyway? It's only natural, then, that the business world would have a great influence on the way we speak and act, not only while at work but also at home.

We need to be wary, though, of workplace language trends because people in business tend to focus on money rather than on people and try to hide any negativity inside of sterilized phrases intended to mislead or distract. Sometimes they make politicians seem forthright. Besides, we don't live at work for a reason, so some separation is healthful.

Add Value

How did you *add value* today? Some managers are actually trained to ask that question of employees as a way to ensure that everyone in the company thinks in terms of money (*value*) at all times.

It used to be assumed that creating a good product or serving a client well would eventually mean an improved business and improved profit for the company, so the focus was on producing quality products and providing exceptional service. For companies that now focus on the words *value*, *adding value*, and *value added*, the focus has shifted from making money through good service to merely making money.

Do we want to keep using a phrase that represents that shift?

The Big Picture

People say to me, *Yes, I agree, but you're not seeing the big picture* or *You're right in the short run, but we have to look at the big picture.*

Where is this *big picture* hanging? Is it over a very big sofa at the Guggenheim? I need to see the *big picture*; otherwise, I'm never going to be a smashing success in the business world, especially if I don't want to use the same phrases over and over.

The Bottom Line

The bottom line is a reference to the last line of an accountant's sheet, which, after all of the numbers have been added and subtracted, indicates whether money was made or lost. *The bottom line* is also used as an indication of the final outcome in a series of events or as just a summary of a longer thought.

The reference to money might be fine to continue using in the business world—as long as overuse isn't a concern; otherwise, *the bottom line* is that there are much better phrase choices. Try *the main point* or *in the final analysis* or *the core of the problem is.*

Brought to the Table

It won't be long until all tables in all offices in this country will need to be made of reinforced steel, perhaps even titanium, because of the incredible number of things that are being *brought to the table.* A person with experience *brings a lot to the table*; someone with energy and enthusiasm *brings a lot to the table*; someone with a good college education *brings a lot to the table.*

The problem is that important details, such as a discussion of experience, energy, enthusiasm, and educational background, are lost in a sea of trendy vagueness.

Crunch the Numbers

When I hear a *crunching* sound, I think of potato chips or autumn leaves, not a businessman making a financial analysis. The phrase *crunching the numbers* makes no sense whatsoever, and the fact that it's so widely used is a clear indication that people will repeat anything they hear—even when it makes no sense.

Here's a phrase to use when *crunch the numbers* is said: *Smash this useless phrase.*

Cutting Edge

Most business people like to think of themselves as entrepreneurs, inventing new products and generating new ideas. While that's certainly true in some instances, most businesses are merely doing the same thing in a different way or with a new marketing scheme. They don't like to admit that, though, so they always talk about being on the *cutting edge*, and the fact that the phrase is not the least bit creative (that is, entrepreneurial) seems to be of no concern.

Downsize

If there is anyone who still doesn't know that the word *downsize* is a polite way to say that people are going to be fired, then the person probably has the same sleeping habits as his great-great-grandfather, Rip Van Winkle.

Hundreds of thousands of people have lost jobs during the first few years of the twenty-first century; however, very few have been *fired*. In fact, the term *fired* has now been reserved for those employees who have lost their jobs due to an act of their own negligence.

Downsizing is now a popular way to lose a job, but it's also a word designed by business people to make it sound as if the person on the unemployment line were the unfortunate victim of a random business process rather than someone who lost her job because of an active choice by those in charge. It dehumanizes the process of firing employees, making it easier for businesses to focus exclusively on money without regard for the needs of the workers.

If a company believes strongly enough in the need to reduce the number of workers, then it should be respectful enough to not try to soften the blow—just go back to calling it *firing* rather than *downsizing.*

Downtime

Any time that two normally separate words are combined without a hyphen to create a new word, the new word is probably a trendy creation rather than an actual word. Such newly invented words are hard to define and, therefore, are hard to know how to use properly.

That's certainly the case with *downtime.* In a general sense, it seems to mean a period of time in which a business is paying a production expense but not getting any production. For example, the time in which the assembly line is not operating due to normal maintenance might be referred to as *downtime,* or the time in which employees have a paid break might be referred to as *downtime.*

At the risk of repeating myself (and ending up as an example in Chapter 2), wouldn't it be less confusing to say what we mean rather than invent new words that may or may not say what we intend?

Duplication of Work/Duties

The process of two companies merging has become as common in the business world as day-old pastries in the conference room, and it's a certainty that one of the first items discussed by leaders of the merging companies is the need to eliminate a *duplication of work*. If two firms, each with its own accounting department and human resources department (see entry later in this chapter), become one company, then one staff can handle the workload of the now-single company. In other words, elimination of a *duplication of work* is a subtle way of eliminating jobs.

The same process is at work on a smaller scale within a single business when *eliminating a duplication of duties* is discussed. The company is not interested in making the workday easier for employees; the company is interested in making its payroll lighter by eliminating a job or two.

This is not to say that the process is automatically wrong; however, communicating the process to employees in a more accurate way would be more respectful, such as by saying *We need to lower costs by reducing the workforce*.

Employees deserve to know if the company is trying to eliminate jobs. Maybe instead of a Help Wanted sign, employers should hang an Employees No Longer Needed sign.

Efficiency

Efficiency has always been a part of the business world—and with good reason. A company needs to turn a profit in order to remain solvent, so money and resources cannot be tossed around like boxes on the loading dock of an overnight delivery company. The problem is that *efficiency* doesn't mean what it did in the past, which means that there can be some confusion.

In the business world, *efficiency* used to mean trying to find a way to run a more effective business, and the result was occasionally a reduction in the workforce. Now, however, technological advances and changes in political policies mean that *efficiency*, for many businesses, is used as a sly way of saying that the goal is to eliminate jobs. When the boss talks about the need to be more *efficient*, he typically means that costs need to be reduced, not that a better system needs to be devised.

In other words, *efficiency* often means that employees should keep their résumés up to date.

Going Forward

A group of outside consultants must've decided over espresso and cupcakes that *going forward* (*Going forward, we expect the company to double its current client base*) was a better way to talk about the progression of time in a positive manner than the word *future*. It's new; therefore, it has to be better.

The word *future* has been used effectively for decades, and it'll be effective for decades more, long after *going forward* has become yesterday's trend.

Heads Will Roll

When I hear the phrase *heads will roll*, I think of guillotines and beheadings, which, come to think of it, seems to be a pretty stiff penalty for not getting that report done on time. We can probably find a less melodramatic way to make the point that *There will be serious consequences if proper action isn't taken*.

Human Resources Department

If we could return to the middle of the twentieth century and ask workers what the contrived term *human resources department* would logically mean, a typical response might have been *The human resources department is the place where employees gather the resources necessary to do their jobs.* It would have been inconceivable that *people* would actually be considered the *resource* since, traditionally, a resource has been defined as an inanimate object. (For more on the definition of *resource*, see "People as a Resource," later in this chapter.)

It should be inconceivable—and unacceptable—now, as well.

I Have a Two O'Clock

Think about how much time has been saved in the past few years by people shortening a long, difficult phrase such as *I have a two o'clock **meeting*** to the much simpler phrase *I have a two o'clock.*

Another way to look at it is that meetings have become so frequent that the word *meeting* is no longer needed. The most efficient among us have gone a step further and shortened it to *I have a two.* Soon, we'll just say *I have a . . .* and let everyone guess the rest.

Trendy language and half sentences aren't the best ways to communicate, so let's *add value* (see entry earlier in this chapter) and perceived intelligence by saying the entire sentence.

I Need It Yesterday

Whenever a boss pulls out the ageless and illogical *I need it yesterday* in response to a question about a deadline, the employee should respond with something new and much more logical, such as *I was planning on having it for you by the end of the day, but since the deadline has already passed, I guess I'll take the rest of the day off.*

Laid Off

The few people who have lost jobs in the past few years and weren't *downsized* (see entry earlier in this chapter) were probably *laid off* instead.

In the past, being *laid off* meant a temporary loss of job during a time of financial strain for the company. The expectation was that when business returned to a more profitable level, the job would be offered back to the employee. It was common for the employee to return to work.

In most instances, being *laid off* is now considered a permanent job loss. If it happens because of poor business, then the employer usually dumps the increased work load on the remaining employees rather than adding employees when business increases. It's rare when someone who had been *laid off* is permitted to return to work.

Reserve the term *laid off* for situations that meet the original criteria; otherwise, the hope of returning to work might be given falsely.

Let's Not Get Ahead of Ourselves

After a phrase finds its way into the language, it's often impossible to determine its origin and why it became so popular. That's especially true of boring and innocuous phrases such as *Let's not get ahead of ourselves*.

Let's not get ahead of ourselves wasn't even clever the first time it was said. It's certainly not particularly articulate, meaning that it doesn't express a new idea or an old idea in a clear way. It's not even trendy since it's been around for a long time. It's just a bland way of saying that *We can't move too quickly* or that *We can't focus on the final product before we work on the initial details*.

Inarticulate, bland, and overused—not exactly employee-of-the-month material.

Let's Not Reinvent the Wheel

We may not be able *to reinvent the wheel*, but if we try, we should be able to find a new way of saying *Let's not repeat work that's already been done*.

The Name of the Game Is

I always thought that business was serious—a very serious (at the risk of creating a redundancy) business. As many times as I've heard that *the name of the game is* one thing or another, such as *making money* or *improving the product* or *winning* or *beating the other guy to the punch*, though, I'm beginning to think that business is merely time at the playground with friends.

On the Same Page

The phrase *on the same page* or *checking to see if everyone is on the same page* was, at one point, a modern and articulate way to say *to ensure agreement* or *to make sure that we're looking at it the same way* or *that there's no misunderstanding*. Of course, having a fifteen-inch black-and-white TV was once a modern way to watch television.

Now, it would be more appropriate to ask if we're all *on the same Web page* or if we're all *on the same digital channel*.

On the Same Wavelength

Scientists talk about *wavelengths*—the *wavelength* of light or sound or other things that I've forgotten since I graduated from college. The only wavelength business people care about is the *wavelength* of money, and since money doesn't have a *wavelength*, this business reference can be filed under *W*—for *what not to say*.

People as a Resource

The only thing worse than labeling *people as a resource* is actually treating people as if they were a resource. Natural resources include trees, water, and oil. Man-made resources include plastic, polyester, and Styrofoam. Perhaps it shouldn't be this way; however, resources are typically used and then tossed in a garbage dump.

This dehumanization process—labeling and using *people as a resource*—is important in the world of business. Employees are trained to expect less since they're merely a *resource,* and it's easier for businesses to take advantage of workers if they consider workers as future trash rather than as human beings.

Workers should no longer accept being labeled as a resource, and people in business should stop labeling workers as such.

Play Hardball

It's ironic that so many business people *play hardball* all the time because most companies have a difficult time fielding a beer league softball team that even can win as many games as it loses. Find a less trite and more precise way of saying that we're going to be tough and do whatever it takes in order to accomplish a goal.

Put It/Us on the Map

Based on the number of products and companies that have been *put on the map* during the last decade or two, being a cartographer must be a much more difficult job than it was in the past.

Ramp Up

Ramp up has become a popular way to say *increase* or *intensify,* such as *We're going to have to ramp up production in order to meet our deadline.* Let's try to *ramp down* this phrase—the last thing we need is another *up* word or phrase. (See "Overuse of Prepositions," in Chapter 1.)

The original use of the phrase seems to be in the world of automobiles. Cars are often *ramped up*, which seems to mean they're engineered to go faster. Slang is common for that type of word usage (it used to be called *souped up*), but as happens too often, the slang has started to run rampant in other areas, too, including business and weather.

It's too 1990s to say *We need to increase production*, so we now say *We need to ramp up production*. It's too boring to say *increase our market share* when we can say *ramp up our business*. It's too articulate to say *The storm is going to strengthen* (or *intensify*), so we say *The storm is going to ramp up* instead.

Ramped up is not just slang but inarticulate, trendy slang. It seems to me that what really needs to be *ramped up* is our vocabulary.

Reach Out

Reach out is a rare example of when the user of the new, trendy phrase isn't trying to sound more intelligent since the old ways of communicating the thought sounded better and were more accurate. *Communicating, talking,* and *making an initial contact* are all more descriptive than *reaching out*.

Reach out and grab one of the more descriptive phrases.

Rising Through the Ranks

Until employees start being promoted from the mail room to sergeant to vice president to colonel, perhaps it would be best to leave the expression *rising through the ranks* to the military.

Run with That/It'll Never Fly/
Are We on the Right Track?

Ideas may indeed shift from a static thought to an active process, but our transportation obsession—as in *Run with that*, *It'll never fly*, and *Are we on the right track?*—is a bit much! All we need is a car reference, and we'll have *Planes, Trains, and Automobiles—The Catalog of Overused Phrases*.

How about *That idea will never make it to the speed limit* or *That's as good as a convertible on the first warm spring day*?

The alternative is to say what we mean in plain English.

Skill Set

Certain jargon makes sense. If a company does a particular process on a regular basis, then it might be easier to create a shortened version of the description of the process instead of continuing to repeat a long description all day every day.

Some expressions, such as *skill set*, aren't jargon; they're merely an attempt to sound more professional or more contemporary by using new words to describe an old idea. The risk is that asking *What kind of a skill set does she bring to the table?* rather than *What are her qualifications?* can sound more flaky and trendy than professional.

Take It to the Next Level

In the world of business, there are three basic levels: loses money, breaks even, and makes money. As a result, we have to keep *taking it to the next level*; otherwise, the boss won't be able to buy her second Bentley—but can't we find another way of saying it?

Actually, it's not that there are so many different levels in the business world but that it has become a trendy, inarticulate way to use the phrase *take it to the next level* to explain degrees of anything. For example, *steps that need to be taken* are called *levels* and *the need to maximize profits* means that *It needs to be taken to the next level*.

The phrase isn't overused just in the world of business but has spread to our everyday lives. Rather than the *need to play better in order to beat the other team in a playground basketball game*, we need to *take our game to the next level*. Rather than *taking the next step in a relationship*, we have to *take it to the next level*.

Being more articulate should result in greater success, both at work and at home.

That Idea Has Legs

Wait, we *got ahead of ourselves* (see entry earlier in this chapter); we shouldn't have *crunched any numbers* yet (see entry earlier in this chapter). We have to first see if *that idea has legs*.

I know that some people believe that ideas are tangible, but I doubt that even those people mean that *ideas have legs*. What was wrong with old reliable standard English expressions such as *That's a good idea* or *That idea is worth pursuing*? Why does an idea have to now have legs? I guess if *the idea is legless*, then there is no use in crunching numbers. If *the idea has legs*, then we'd better move quickly; otherwise, it might walk to our competitors.

Time Is Money

If we're going to use the expression *time is money* from the perspective of the business world, where it is most commonly used, then we need to understand that the origin of the phrase is based on the premise that *money* is a commodity that is at least as valuable as *time*. And according to most business people, *money* is even more valuable than *time*.

Money more valuable than time? That's ridiculous. Time is always more important, like lunchtime, vacation time, and overtime!

We're Going to Have to Let You Go

We're going to have let you go was a classic dismissal line the first time it was used, which probably explains its ongoing popularity. What if the person doesn't want to be *let go*? The company obviously doesn't want to fire the person since the employer is making it sound as though it were not his idea, so ask the employee. Maybe he'd like to continue to work until he has enough money to retire, or perhaps she would like to earn enough money to pay her bills this month.

Firing someone is an aggressive act; it cannot be turned into a passive-aggressive act merely to ease the conscience of the employer.

Why Don't You Go Ahead and . . .

Can you imagine Dr. Phil saying to someone *Why don't you go ahead and come in on Saturday and work on that report?* No, of course you can't. Dr. Phil is not a weasel. He's a confident man, and confident people say things directly.

Trying to make it sound as though it were the other person's idea, which is what the wording *Why don't you go ahead and come in on Saturday* is trying to accomplish, is being manipulative. I'm not asking you to do it; I'm not telling you to do it; it's *your* idea.

If it's not deliberately manipulative, which it probably is since managers usually understand the rules of communication, then it's passive-aggressive. Rather than just saying what is meant because it might not be received well, the speaker tries to say it as though it were an innocent request instead of what he's really doing, which is forcing the employee to sacrifice his day off.

Dr. Phil would probably just say something similar to *I need the report by Monday at 10 a.m.* and let the staffer decide how to get it done. It's always better to be direct, so we should avoid the indirect *Why don't you go ahead and* at all times.

You Thought You Were Clever, But . . .
PHRASES THAT MAY HAVE
BEEN WITTY THE FIRST TIME
THEY WERE USED

The entries in this chapter make me wonder about our collective sanity. We all know how incredibly frustrating it is when we hear a predictable and time-wasting response during normal conversation or after asking a simple question. But when it's our turn to respond to the same topics, we often say the same things in the same way!

Perhaps the response was, indeed, witty and charming the first time it was used, but for some reason, the charm has been lost over the last couple of million repetitions.

No one can execute these with any style at this point, and you're not the lone exception to the rule.

Are We Having Fun Yet?

Are we having fun yet? is sarcastic—not in a good way but in a tired, worn-out, never-say-it-again kind of way. This phrase is as useful as a hole-ridden sock that's lying in a mud puddle in the gutter of a soot-covered city street, and saying *Are we having fun yet?* should be as tempting as it would be to bend over, pick up the sock, wring out the water, and slide it onto your foot.

Don't you know whether you're having a good time? Do you really need to ask someone else whether *we*, which obviously includes *you*, are having fun yet? Of course not—because the question is being used as a way to taunt someone who is clearly not having a good time. It's said to a co-worker who just found out that her computer lost all of the data she's been working on for six months. It's sometimes said to a waiter or waitress by a customer at a bar, as though the worker should join his group's leisure. Don't taunt. Be polite, and tip well.

Sometimes it's used as a lame attempt to join a larger group. Perhaps a college student will ask *Are we having fun yet?* as he sits down and joins classmates in a study session before the biggest exam of the semester. A good lesson to learn would be to not speak for everyone else. A boss might awaken from his late-morning nap, wander out of his office to where everyone has been working for hours, and ask *Are we having fun yet?* Bosses aren't supposed to fit in.

And sometimes, it's said because the person doesn't know what else to say. Here's one phrase you won't hear me ridicule in this book: Silence is golden.

Are You Working Hard or Hardly Working?/Say One for Me While You're Down There

As someone whose first job was in a grocery store, the comments *Are you working hard or hardly working?* and *Say one for me while you're down there* are merely a small sampling of the types of things that you can say to a worker that will make him want to quit his job and move into the vast wilderness to live alone for the rest of his days.

When I was an employee-of-the-month-caliber grocery clerk, twenty minutes was the average interval between one *Are you working hard or hardly working?* and the next. It is surprising that after about twenty such comments per day, five days per week, the charm is lost. *Say one for me while you're down there* wasn't said nearly as often—not because it's more clever or used in a more discerning manner but because grocery clerks spend only part of the day kneeling in front of the shelves. Shoppers have to time that one.

I understand that we want to be friendly, and it's hard to generate new material every day, but that's the beauty of the *Hi, how are ya?* It's simple, to the point, and, in most cases, rhetorical. It can even be personalized by actually pronouncing the word *you*.

Don't Let the Door Hit You on the Way Out

Don't let your mind think of anything new to say and utter a *Don't let the door hit you on the way out.*

Gender Humor

We're now in the twenty-first century, and family roles are not limited to the nice, neat packages of the past. In case you hadn't noticed, many married women work now; that's been going on for only the past forty or fifty years, so I can see why people still make the same gender jokes that were popular when a husband brought his boss home for martinis and a dinner that took the "Mrs." all afternoon to prepare. Anyone remember Laura Petrie?

In most homes, both spouses work. In other homes, children are raised by single parents—usually a woman but sometimes a man. And some families consist of, or are headed by (note to people in the red states: You may want to cover your eyes), two people of the same sex.

As a result, jokes about the *wife being such a bad cook that she can't boil water* or the *husband not doing anything around the house except emptying the trash and walking the dog* or the *wife needing both large closets and three of the four dresser drawers for her clothes while the husband's clothes are squeezed into the file cabinet* are not only trite but horribly outdated.

It makes me wonder whether some of us are having a difficult time adjusting.

Height Humor

Different people have different opinions about what's funny or clever and why. The key is delivery or timing or a sense of the absurd; however, no one believes that the key to being funny is pointing out a person's most obvious physical attribute. For that reason, we should not make jokes about height to people who are either exceptionally tall or exceptionally short. It's not a matter of being politically correct; it's hard to imagine that the person wants to hear what you have to say about something he or she has been well aware of ever since first grade when the mocking started.

As a result, don't even think about saying the following: *Hi, Stretch, how's the weather up there? Do you play basketball? Hi, Shorty, how's the weather down there? If you need a boost to get on the sofa, let me know.*

The same goes for fat and thin jokes. Being thin in our ever-growing (if you know what I mean) country is usually a source of envy and, therefore, is not considered funny by most Americans. We also have an understanding that it's hurtful to make weight jokes to an overweight person, so we don't—we usually save those for behind the person's back.

I Could Tell You, But Then I'd Have to Kill You

I could tell you, but then I'd have to kill you is a predictable line that is usually reserved for second-rate spy movies. If you want to emulate characters from the movies, then at least pick *quality* movies.

I Don't Care What Joe Says About You; You're All Right in My Book

I don't care what anyone says—the phrase *I don't care what* [name] *says about you; you're all right in my book* is too outdated and lacking in creativity to be all right in my book.

I Feel Your Pain

The phrase *I feel your pain* isn't overused to the point of annoyance, but because it's associated with President Bill Clinton and the 1990s, it's a good example of a statement that represents a trend of yesteryear that is now outdated. You may as well ask, *Did you catch the* Arsenio Hall Show *last night?*

If You Believe That One, Then I Have Some Land in Florida/a Bridge in Brooklyn to Sell You

The real estate market is booming. All the *swamps in Florida* have been drained so that extravagant condominiums for retired New Yorkers can sprout. The *Brooklyn Bridge* is worth millions, and it's not for sale anyway. So unless you're trying to make someone rich, don't use any version of this, including the abbreviated and unfinished version that many of us say for the purpose of word economy: *If you believe that one . . .*

Let's see, now that oil companies have been given free reign to drill in Alaska, we might try: *If you believe that one, then I have some unspoiled land in Alaska to sell you.*

I'll Have My People Call Your People

If you look at historical time lines, many things are easy to date. The Declaration of Independence was signed in 1776; Alexander Graham Bell invented the telephone in 1876; and the British Invasion started when a few English men got off a plane in the early 1960s. What's less clear is when eras end; therefore, no one can say with any certainty when the era of the entourage ended, but it's over now. We can all stop pretending that we have *people*. Besides, almost everyone has a cell phone, so there is no need to drag a third party into the mix by declaring, *I'll have my people call your people*. All that does is increase the chance of roaming charges.

In-Law Jokes

Take my mother-in-law jokes. Please.

We're all tired of in-law jokes. It's difficult for jokes about unfamiliar people to be funny in the first place, and we don't know your in-laws—and, frankly, based on what you've been saying about them, we don't want to.

Generic jokes about groups of people are just that—generic, which means that they aren't funny.

It's Hard Work, But Someone Has to Do It

As a general rule, if a phrase is so popular that it doesn't need to be completed in order to be understood, then it's time for the phrase to go to that great dictionary in the sky. *It's hard work, but someone has to do it* has become so predictable that it is often just shortened to *It's hard work, but* without the dazzling finale.

Rest in peace.

It's Not What You Say but How You Say It

It's not what you say but how you say it—umm, it's actually both; otherwise, I wouldn't have written this book. You probably agree; otherwise, you wouldn't be reading this book.

Just Say No

Kiss my grits; Whatcha talkin' 'bout, Willis; and *Where's the beef?* are all as timely and clever as Nancy Reagan's anti-drug campaign slogan, *Just say no.* If your clever catchphrases are twenty-five years old, then I'd hate to look in your underwear drawer.

Kids, Don't Try This at Home

As television programs became more and more sensational (even before the day of the reality show), television executives had a choice. They could choose to create shows that didn't put people at risk of losing their health or their lives, or they could put a disclaimer such as *Don't try this at home* on the bottom of the screen so that they didn't get sued by the survivors or the maimed. The decision was simple: ratings over common sense.

I'll admit that the first couple of times that this was mocked in real life, it was funny. For example, a co-worker might say *Don't try this at home* right before gluing papers to the boss's desk while he was away at a convention in Detroit.

No one is amused any longer—and security cameras are everywhere.

No, I Got 'Em All Cut

Responding with *No, I got 'em all cut* is an answer only a third-grader could love. Of course, asking *Did you get your hair cut?* is a question that only a fifth-grader would think was appropriate to ask. Unless asking people whether they trimmed their toenails or shaved their legs seems appropriate, then both the question and answer no longer need to be used.

No Pun Intended

The percentage of times that someone says *no pun intended* when no pun was actually intended is roughly 0.05 percent. The other 99.95 percent of the time, the speaker is trying to make sure that the listener understands that what she just said was clever.

Let us discover your cleverness without any hints.

That's What She Said

Using the response *That's what she said* to (or about) anything that could possibly be interpreted as a sexual reference is as outdated as it is uncouth and immature. As a result, its use should be restricted to the privacy of your own room.

I know. I know. *Restricted for the privacy of your own room—that's what she said.* And, in this instance, I couldn't agree with her more.

Weather Humor

Based on the number of jokes, weather forecasting must be the most ridiculed job anyone could ever have. Humor about anything is good, but all weather jokes fall into a few boring, predictable categories.

The undependability of weather forecasts is one category. People say, for example, *I know it's going to rain on Saturday because they're forecasting sunshine* to the bank teller, who, I'm sure, doesn't get tired of talking about the weather to a hundred customers a day. Actually, maybe the tellers don't mind since they're always asking *What's it like out there?* or *Is it still cold?* as often as customers are complaining about the bad forecast.

It's even worse when people personalize the unpredictability of the weather, as in *I'm sure the forecast for Saturday is going to be wrong because it always rains on my birthday*. Strangers or acquaintances don't know you well enough to understand your self-deprecating humor.

The other standard jokes are about how *I can forecast the weather, too: I just look out the window* or how the weatherman has the only job in which he can be wrong half the time and still get paid.

I'm not proposing that we stop making jokes about the weather; otherwise, advertising executives, sitcom writers, and the rest of us would have to think of something new to talk about. We just need new jokes.

What Are You Up To?

If there were a lack-of-cleverness scale for answers that paralleled the Richter scale for earthquakes, then giving your height in response to being asked *What are you up to?* would be equivalent to the earthquake that is going to make Las Vegas beachfront property.

Whatever Floats Your Boat

Water floats every boat, so it's hard to even imagine why anyone ever thought *Whatever floats your boat* was a clever response, let alone why anyone would still think it is.

Wouldn't You Like to Know?

Answering a legitimate question with the sometimes teasing and sometimes flirtatious *Wouldn't you like to know?* is as tired as it is uninformative. Unless you're destined to become the next big sex symbol, just answer the question.

Yep, All Day

Responding with *Yep, all day* when asked the date was popular in high school, and I thought we'd have outgrown it by college. We didn't, and now, more than twenty-five years after graduating from college, believe it or not, I still hear this phrase all too often.

It's time to lobby Congress to pass a law stating that everyone must wear a watch with a calendar.

9

That's Not What I Meant
INARTICULATE LANGUAGE

Many words and phrases do not express what we're trying to say, at least not as well as we might like. One of the main reasons for the lack of effective expression is that we tend to rely on old and trusted phrases rather than honest words and emotions.

It's hard to imagine a less effective way of communicating an event of any importance than by using a cliché, catchphrase, or overused quip. That would be like starting a great art collection with a $5 Picasso poster rather than an original work.

All Things Considered

The phrase *all things considered* indicates that something was done only after all possibilities had been considered. If that were truly the case—if we had actually taken the time to consider everything—then isn't it likely that we would have come up with an original way of saying it, at least once in a while?

By the way, saying *all in all* instead of *all things considered* is not an improvement. I think that *all in all* is supposed to mean the same thing, but it really doesn't say much.

Bang for Your Buck

I don't know about getting your money's worth with the phrase *bang for your buck*, but we certainly get a lot of *slang for our dollar* with the phrase. If we stopped long enough to think about what we were saying, we would certainly conclude that it's too informal and foolish for use outside of our own homes. Try saying *get the most for our money* or *getting a good deal* or *the best quality for the price we're paying*.

Bored to Death

Boring and *death* are two things that should come to mind when someone says *bored to death*. We should all be *bored* of hearing the phrase and agree to put it to *death*. *Bored to tears* deserves the same fate, and we will soon find out how I feel about as *boring as hell* (see "Hell," later in this chapter).

Bring It On

The phrase *bring it on* (or the shortened *bring it*) indicates bravado rather than communicates anything of substance. Unless being reactionary rather than explanatory is your style of communication, use words that explain yourself more effectively.

Don't Go There

Seldom do good communication skills include veiled threats, which is the category in which *don't go there* belongs. Find a better way to express displeasure when a topic is broached that you're not interested in discussing. Try something like *I'd rather not talk about that*, or have an answer or action prepared for the inevitable question of *Or else what?*

Evil-Doer

Evil-doer is too simplistic and general to be of any specific use. Using such a term means that either the speaker (perhaps a politician of note) is unable to articulate in an adequate manner or that the speaker (perhaps a politician of note or his speech writer) believes the audience is not bright enough to deal with detailed facts.

Hell

Some people like to say *It's as boring as hell*, but they're obviously not talking about the weather since we hear both *It's as hot as hell* and, ironically, *It's as cold as hell*. Also, *It's as windy as hell*, which might help when it's hot. *It rained like hell*, but somehow it's also *as dry as hell*. This is not to mention that *It snowed like hell* and *It stormed like hell*.

People have *dates from hell*, which might have included the ever-popular *movie from hell*. Many of us have had *hellish days* and equally *hellish nights*. Unpleasant birthdays, bad work days, poor haircuts, and even good times (*hell of a good time*) are all sent compliments of Lucifer, who, to his credit, doesn't seem to let the weather stop him.

If you want to adequately emphasize any experience, then don't use the word *hell*. As an adjective, the word has lost all effectiveness.

Hot

Rarely is one generation's trendy word or expression repeated by the following generation, but for some reason, using the word *hot* to describe a person's looks has survived for a couple of generations. That's too bad. Unless you want to sound like an eighteen-year-old in heat, there are certainly more complimentary and respectful ways of indicating that someone is attractive.

I Don't See Myself . . .

Any athlete or entertainer who speaks of himself or herself in the third person is instantly mocked—and with good reason. It sounds ridiculous for Bob, the superstar football player to say, *I think Bobby is going to have a tremendous season* when talking about himself.

Is it much different when we say things such as *I don't see myself working for this company five years from now*? The only possible reason for speaking about yourself in the same way in which you'd talk about a different person is that you've learned to do so through repetition. It's more effective to say what you mean; try *I don't anticipate working here five years from now* or *I doubt I'll still be at this company in five years.*

I Have a Lot on My Plate

No one is *too busy* any longer; that's not trendy enough. No one *participates in many different activities*; that's too bland. No one has *too much work to do*; that's 1980s-speak. Everyone, however, has a *lot on his or her plate.*

That covers every imaginable situation yet says nothing—although it might explain the country's growing obesity problem.

I'm in Way Over My Head

Swimming might be the best overall exercise since it combines aerobic exercise with resistance training. Maybe people think if they use a swimming reference—more accurately, a swimming-not-very-well reference—then they'll get the benefits of swimming without having dry skin and hair that smells like chlorine.

Otherwise, we would find a better way of expressing that we feel overwhelmed by a task or situation than *always* picking *I'm in way over my head.* Try *I don't know what I'm doing* or *I'm afraid that this might be too hard for me* or even *Help!*

Is This a Great Country, or What?

There are no multiple choices for answering *Is this a great country, or what?* It's rhetorical.

Saying *Is this a great country, or what?* in a sarcastic way in a discussion about a problem related to society or politics is an ineffective expression since it says nothing. It is an effective way, however, to express apathy, which might be part of the problem in the first place.

Occasionally, *Is this a great country, or what?* is used as a way of expressing having gotten away with something. A person pulled over for driving seventy-five in a fifty-five-miles-per-hour zone might say *Is this a great country, or what?* when recounting the story of how mentioning that his cousin is a detective in the police force allowed him to receive a warning instead of an expensive ticket.

Responding with *This is the greatest country in the world* any time a discussion about society or politics erupts isn't any better. The belief that the country is great is a widely shared opinion and perfectly reasonable; what's not reasonable is a refusal to even consider the possibility that a problem might exist in society or politics. The way to keep a country great is for its citizens to monitor its actions in order to ensure that the country is on the correct path rather than defensively dismissing any possible challenge as being preposterous merely because something negative was said about the country.

It Blew Me Away/I'm Blown Away

Most overused phrases have a history of logic behind them. For instance, *It was a nightmare* (see later in this chapter) makes sense as a way to describe something that is frightening since nightmares are also frightening. It's not the phrase itself that's ineffective but, rather, the *overuse* of the phrase that renders it ineffective; however, *It blew me away* and *I'm blown away* have never made any sense—unless your goal is to sound like Wayne and Garth from *Wayne's World*, that is.

These are ridiculous slang phrases that are too casual, outdated, and illogical for use in any situation outside of a cable-access channel (or the twenty-first-century version, a streaming video feed) that originates in your parents' basement.

It Makes Me Sick

If people didn't eat everything that was on their plates, which, as I discussed previously (see "I Have a Lot on My Plate" earlier in this chapter), are so obviously overloaded, then perhaps fewer people would get sick when they experience ordinary things—for example, *He has so much money, it makes me sick* or *She's so self-centered, it makes me sick* or *Just the sight of him makes me sick.*

It makes me sick is said so often that I wish I hadn't had that third taco at dinner. I'm not feeling well.

It Was a Nightmare

It was a nightmare is one of the most eye-rolling phrases in the English language. Rather than creating the desired effect of describing a frightening event or situation, overuse of the phrase in mundane or boring situations has resulted in a phrase that reeks of melodrama.

I Want It So Bad I Can Almost Taste/Feel/ Smell/Touch It

Picture the best job imaginable—six-figure salary, great benefits, and twelve weeks of vacation every year. When your spouse asks about the potential job, the only thing that separates you from a snappy description is filling in the blank toward the end of the prefabricated sentence, *I want it so bad that I can _____ it.*

Do you go with the most popular *taste* or the nearly as popular *feel* or *smell*? Or do you choose the slightly more obscure *touch*? In the end, it doesn't really matter which is selected since all of them are so overused that it will sound like just another dead-end job.

I Was on the Edge of My Seat

As the use of the phrase *I was on the edge of my seat* has spread from describing movie viewing to describing ordinary life, it has lost its ability to adequately describe a feeling of suspense. Imagining a person in a theater who is literally on the edge of his seat paints a visual image of suspense; it works. Imagining someone on the edge of her sofa or bed doesn't work, though, since that's not how people normally react to a suspenseful book or movie while at home.

As with many of the entries in this chapter, the original use of the phrase was effective—and the phrase might still be effective if it hadn't spread into other areas.

I've Never Seen Anything Like That in My Life/ That's the Worst Thing I've Ever Seen

The phrase *I've never seen anything like that in my life* seldom provides the emphasis intended.

Using the phrase for ordinary events unfairly limits your life. If it's said when it rains heavily, when a baseball player hits a long home run, and when a soufflé falls, then people listening are forced to conclude that your life is uneventful since trivial occurrences are what you choose to gauge your life by.

Conversely, using the phrase to describe something absolutely incredible, such as the destruction of seventy-three homes in your neighborhood by a flash flood, understates the description of the event. It is assumed that no ordinary person would see the complete demolition of a neighborhood by a flash flood on two separate occasions, so saying *I've never seen anything like it in my life*, although accurate, does little to describe the situation.

Personalizing an event that is not of personal concern, such as *That was the worst car accident I've ever seen*, is also not an effective way to communicate. It shifts the focus from where it ought to be—in this case, the people involved in the accident—to the speaker.

We all love you, but not everything is about you!

Monumental Decision

If there's one way of ensuring that an important *decision* will be trivial, or at least seem trivial, then it's to use the word *monumental* as the adjective to describe nearly every *decision* that's ever made.

Seldom have two useful words been combined to create a more trite phrase. If we're honest with ourselves, we each probably have five or six truly monumental decisions during the course of our entire lives; however, we throw the phrase around five or six times per week. Leave the drama to the afternoon soap operas.

More Money Than God

We live in a country of religious freedom, so everyone has the right to believe whatever he would like; however, it's hard to imagine a situation in which anyone's God would collect money.

When I hear the phrase *more money than God*, I imagine God asking St. Paul if he has any spare change so He can finish his penny rolls.

Real

When I hear *I had a real nice time tonight*, I envision the Old West, with a cowgirl saying that to a cowboy to end a date right before she jumps off his horse and runs into the log cabin. *Real* means that it actually happened or that it's true: *That's a real story* or *That's a real orange—not a plastic one. Real* is not an acceptable substitute for *very*.

The word *really*, since it means truly, is a better substitute; however, I'm suspicious that *really* might be a reflection of trying to improve on the mistake of substituting *real* for *very* by trying to transform *real* into an adverb by adding *-ly*. Besides, *really* is overused and *real* informal, so it's best avoided.

While I'm on the subject, asking *Are you for real?* or answering a question with *For real* is slang, which means, of course, that it shouldn't be used.

Stranger Things Have Happened

Stranger things have happened might still be an acceptable phrase for expressing a glimmer of hope if it were ever used accurately; however, it's almost exclusively said when an outcome has already been determined, and there is no reason for any hope.

In sports, for example, when the team that is trailing by three touchdowns recovers a fumble with one minute left in the game, a fan might say *stranger things have happened* about a potential comeback. In life, after spending a dollar and picking nine numbers between zero and a hundred, a man might say to his wife *stranger things have happened* when discussing their chances of winning the Super Mega 6-State Jackpot that is worth $400,000,000.

In most instances, when the phrase is used, stranger things

have *not* happened, which means that what's *strange* is that we keep saying it.

That's the Stupidest Thing I've Ever Seen/ Done/Heard

Every day, the world is full of people who have done the *stupidest things they've ever done* or seen the *stupidest things they've ever seen* or heard the *stupidest things they've ever heard*. Since it happens each day, what's occurring today is even *stupider* than what occurred yesterday; therefore, the level of stupidity must be continually increasing!

Technically, the phrases are also wrong because *stupider* and *stupidest* aren't even words (see "Stupidest," in Chapter 1); however, since we keep getting *stupider* and *stupider,* that might not be a distinction worth making for much longer.

They Say/You Know What They Say

We've all made the standard jokes in response to someone saying *They say that* or *You know what they say*: **They** *must be very smart; after all,* **they** *seem to know everything. Who are these people who think they know everything?* For some reason, understanding how ineffective the phrase is when others use it never stops us from saying *They say that* or *You know what they say* to someone else.

Saying something that will leave us exposed to being mocked is similar to eating M&M's candies. We buy the bag knowing that we shouldn't. When we get home, we think we're going to just have one serving—one measly ounce never hurt anyone. We might even measure the one ounce and put the candy into a bowl so that we're not tempted to have more. Once the bag is open, though, we keep eating until all that's left in the bottom of the bag is a few sweet, chocolaty crumbs.

The best way to keep from eating the entire bag is to leave the bag on the store shelf, and the best way to avoid being mocked for saying *They say* or *You know what they say* is to keep your lips locked. Hey, wait, I guess that would work for the candy, too.

This Rocks

Nothing says metal-head quite like *This rocks*; in fact, saying it is the verbal equivalent of having over-teased hair halfway down your back while walking along the street playing air guitar. That's not to imply that there's anything wrong with that type of music or with those who listen to it; however, the metal-head image isn't one normally associated with personal, professional, or monetary success, so you may want to keep this phrase locked in your guitar case in the basement.

Tornado Sounded Like a Freight Train

Does a freight train sound so much different from a passenger train that the people in tornado alley can tell the difference? It certainly seems that way since every witness of every tornado in the past two decades has said *The tornado sounded like a freight train*.

What's Up?/Hey!

It's time for a multiple-choice quiz. (There might be more than one correct answer.) Which of the following greetings are proper in all situations?

A. Hello.
B. Hi. How are you?
C. Good morning.
D. *What's up?*
E. *Hey!*
F. All of the above.
G. None of the above.

If you answered *Hello* thinking that *Good morning* was a trick answer because the question didn't mention the time of day, then skip ahead to the next question.

If your answer included *What's up?* or *Hey!* then you need to take a course in remedial manners.

If you answered *All of the above* or *None of the above*, then you may as well put the book down and turn the television back on because you weren't even trying.

When It's All Said and Done

It's a shame that the phrase *less talk, more action* is probably almost as trite and ineffective as the phrase *when it's all said and done*; otherwise, that would be my recommendation.

Actually, I suspect that *when it's all said and done* is a close cousin to the more modern phrase *at the end of the day* since both phrases basically mean *at the conclusion* or *when everything has been decided*. Of course, the main thing that's *done* (as in finished), when *it's all been said*, is the effectiveness of the phrase.

10

Insincerity Is the Highest Form of Flattery
INSINCERE OR DISMISSIVE PHRASES

To quote a famous line, *Insincerity is the highest form of flattery.* Oh wait; it's not *insincerity* but *imitation* that's the compliment. That's too bad because if it were insincerity, then we'd be complimenting each other all the time.

When we're trying to give advice, commiserate, or share a life experience by spitting out an old and trusted axiom rather than dealing with the specific topic, the result is often the appearance of insincerity or of being dismissive.

That's not going to help anyone—or your reputation.

At Your Earliest Convenience

Too informal is almost always a problem; however, certain phrases, such as *at your earliest convenience*, are too formal. Perhaps it's not the formality that makes the phrase seem so insincere— perhaps it's just because it's another overused phrase.

Regardless, unless sounding superior or maintaining distance from others is the goal, it's better just to say *as soon as possible* or *when you can get to it*.

Don't Hesitate to Call

There seem to be only two instances in which the phrase *Don't hesitate to call* is meant with any sincerity. One is when it's seems obvious that a call will not be needed. For example, after a repairman finishes a job and thinks everything is fine and the customer is happy, he'll often say, *If you have any questions, don't hesitate to call*. If he thinks there might be a problem, then chances are that he'll toss the bill on the floor as he runs toward the door.

The other instance is when the person saying *Don't hesitate to call* believes that the person will need to call only once. She certainly doesn't mind one call, but she's not too happy about a second. For example, after a lengthy appointment with a concerned patient, the doctor will often say *Don't hesitate to call*. The first time the patient calls the doctor, the doctor gives free advice. The second time, though, the answering service picks up and recommends calling the office early Monday morning.

Unless you actually want someone to call, don't make the offer.

Don't Sweat It
Unless you know how effective a person's antiperspirant is or you want to sound like a Quaalude-carrying hippie from the 1970s, stay away from the phrase *Don't sweat it*.

God Works in Mysterious Ways/It's All Part of God's Plan
Although it may at times be hard to tell in this country, not everyone believes in the same God or believes in God at all. That should be reason enough to limit the use of the phrases *God works in mysterious ways* and *It's all part of God's plan* as ways of giving advice or commiserating with someone. If the listener is not of the same faith or doesn't believe that God's will supersedes his own free will, then the listener might be offended by the preaching quality of the response.

Even if the religion side of the equation is not a problem, these phrases are downright dismissive. If someone is trying to have a serious discussion about an important or emotional event in his life, such as the loss of a job or the death of a friend, then just chalking it up to God's will, while perhaps an honest response from the speaker, will be of no practical use to the listener.

Good for You
Good for you, at least in our society, is too often said in an insincere way to ever be safely used as a sincere expression.

In some instances, the person is using the phrase sarcastically, such as saying *Good for you* in response to someone excitedly announcing that he just bought a new coffeemaker. At other times, it is said in a poor attempt to hide jealousy, such as saying *Good for you* when someone buys a new car but the speaker is still driving his parent's Pinto.

Strive for sincerity, or at least be creative if choosing the always popular sarcasm.

Have a Nice Day

If there were royalties paid for the inventor of phrases, then the evil person who "invented" the fake sunshine-in-a-line phrase *Have a nice day* would now have control over every bit of money on the planet.

The only way to stop the evil is to stop using the sentence.

I Know How You Feel, But . . .

It seems as if *I know how you feel* is followed by a *but* nearly every time it's mentioned, which makes me think that the person might not be trying to be agreeable as much as persuasive.

For example, if a loved one says *I'm so disappointed that I didn't get that job; it makes me feel like a failure,* responding with *I know how you feel, but the next job will work out* is a way of telling the person that you don't understand how she feels. It's not about whether the next opportunity will work out; it's about how missing this opportunity made her feel. At the very least, it's a way of trying to convince the person to not feel that way any longer.

I'll Be Forever in Your Debt

Forever is a very long time to owe anyone for anything, which is why it's so surprising that people use the phrase *I'll be forever in your debt* so often.

Send a thank-you note and a bottle of wine, or return the favor at the next opportunity, but enough with the lifelong promise of servitude.

I Love You Sooooo Much/I'm Sooooo Glad to See You/You're the Bessssst Friend I've Ever Had

A melodrama watch is now in effect. Remember, a *warning* is different from a *watch*. A *watch* means that melodrama is possible, and a *warning* means that melodrama is already occurring. This is only a watch. If a melodrama warning is issued, then you will be instructed on what to do.

When a person adds extra emphasis to something, it means one of three things: Either the person would like to become an actor on a soap opera or is compensating for something he doesn't really believe or is trying to look a certain way for someone else's benefit. Sincere expressions of emotion are rarely expressed in a dramatic way; they're usually expressed in a, well, sincere way.

That's the reason that sentences such as *I love you sooooo much* or *I'm sooooo glad to see you* or *You're the bessssst friend I've ever had* warrant further analysis. If they're not used in dramatic situations, such as when lovers reconnect after a long absence or when the fire department arrives or when someone just threw himself in front of a bullet to save a friend, then the melodrama watch should be upgraded to a warning.

When a melodrama warning is issued, roll your eyes; then, turn and walk away.

I'm Glad to Hear That

I'm glad to hear that has some of the same problems as *Good for you* (see earlier in this chapter). It's often used to express sarcasm, but rather than hiding jealousy, it tends to personalize the experience too much.

When someone is talking about something that happened in his life—something that affects him and not you, such as a new job—there has to be a better way of expressing excitement or support rather than drawing yourself into the discussion. Instead of *I'm glad to hear that*, it might be better to say *You must be thrilled. I know you've wanted that job for a long time.*

There are exceptions to every rule, of course, and I'd make an exception if the friend won millions of dollars in the lottery. Do whatever you can to attract attention to yourself in order to be generously rewarded around the holidays.

I'm Sorry If Anyone Was Offended

We often hear an athlete who makes a racist or homophobic comment to the press, a movie star who publicly embarrasses herself, or a politician who lets an unpopular opinion slip without its typical coating of doublespeak say *I'm sorry if anyone was offended* instead of the more appropriate *I'm sorry for my behavior.*

The phrase shifts the responsibility from the speaker to the listener because the person listening must decide whether he or she was offended and whether an apology is therefore warranted. The person whose behavior was potentially offensive is, then, largely relieved of responsibility. On the other hand, *I'm sorry for my behavior* means that *Whether or not anyone was offended, I realize that my behavior was unacceptable*. All responsibility is on the speaker, and none is on the listener—as it should be when trying to apologize.

The difference between *I'm sorry for my behavior* and *I'm sorry if anyone was offended* is the same as the difference between *I'm sorry* and *I'm sorry I got caught*.

It Could Be Worse

Of course, *it could be worse*! Things could almost always be worse. That's not the point. The point, when a person says *It could be worse*, is that *it probably could be better*. In fact, it was probably better five minutes ago, yesterday, or last week; otherwise, the person wouldn't be talking about it now. Responding with *It could be worse* is a good way to sound as though the other person's problem wasn't important. It's the equivalent of saying, *If it gets worse, then let me know; otherwise, I'm not really interested*.

Similarly, following a complaint about your own life with an *Oh well, it could always be worse* is a good way to have your problems dismissed since you don't even seem to be taking them seriously yourself.

It's Always Darkest Before the Dawn

Depending on the moon phases, it's just as dark at midnight or 2 a.m. as it is one minute before the sun begins to rise, so the phrase *It's always darkest before the dawn* is not only an insincere and trite way of saying that things always seem worse right before they start to get better, but it's just plain wrong.

It's Bigger Than Both of Us

Don't be tempted to use a godless version of the phrase *God works in mysterious ways* (see earlier in this chapter), such as *It's bigger than both of us.* That phrase still does not show any concern for or understanding of the specific situation. By more or less saying that it's something we can't understand, you're effectively saying *Don't ask me* or *It's not my problem.*

Try to take into consideration the type of response that might help you deal with a similar situation.

I Wouldn't Worry About That If I Were You

Talk about dismissive: *I wouldn't worry about that if I were you* belongs in the Dismissive Hall of Fame (DHF)! When someone wants to talk about a concern, saying *I wouldn't worry about that if I were you* is the equivalent of saying *You're not smart enough* [or mature enough or logical enough] *to decide for yourself whether you should be concerned about something, so I'll decide for you, and I've decided that this is not something you should worry about.*

Of course, people don't mean to sound this way, which

means it shouldn't be said this way. Find another way of expressing *While I understand your concern, the problem is probably not as bad as you think it is* or *The same thing happened to me, and it turned out fine.*

Either that, or just admit that you want to be in charge of everyone else's emotional life.

Let's Get Together

A denotative definition is the literal definition of the word—the meaning of the word that you would find in the dictionary. A connotative definition is not the literal meaning but, rather, what the word might imply. For instance, the word *rest* means, in a denotative sense, *to recline or rejuvenate.* Used connotatively, it can mean *death,* as in *Rest in peace.*

If we were to apply the words *denotative* and *connotative* to the phrase *Let's get together* for two acquaintances or formerly close friends, it might literally mean that *We should get together for lunch.* Connotatively, however, it means something quite different, specifically, *I know that we haven't seen each other in a while, and it's probably not going to happen soon.*

Reserve *Let's get together for lunch* for instances when you actually want to resume a more personal relationship.

Life Isn't Supposed to Be Easy

Very few people expect that life will always be as easy as turning a profit with inside information on Wall Street. If a person is saying that he expected a particular area of his life to go more smoothly than it has, then the appropriate response would have something to do with that particular area of the person's life rather than the generic *Life isn't supposed to be easy* line.

Besides, perhaps life *is* supposed to be easy!

May I Help You?

Everyone knows by now that customer service personnel in stores are trained to ask *May I help you*, but they should stop saying it unless they mean it.

In fact, based on the surprised look when a customer says something other than *No thanks, I'm just browsing*, it's pretty clear that most customer service representatives consider it to be a rhetorical question.

Only Time Will Tell

Every reasonable person, other than psychics and prophets, understands that the future is yet to be determined, so the brilliant insight *Only time will tell* states the obvious. It adds nothing to the conversation. It does not make the speaker sound astute, and it most certainly does not give the listener the impression that the speaker cares about his or her specific concern.

Stop By and Say Hi Sometime

Inviting someone to *Stop by and say hi* is usually intended in the same manner as *Let's get together* (see earlier in this chapter), only it's more dangerous since you're actually giving the person permission to swing by the house.

Remember, it's easier to screen phone calls than doorbells, so it might be better to use the equally insincere *Give me a call sometime* instead.

You Can't Win 'Em All

No reasonable person believes that she will succeed with every attempt, so telling someone that *You can't win 'em all* is like saying *It's sunny on some days, and it rains on others.* No useful information has been provided. In addition, if the statement is made in response to a particular failed attempt, then the speaker will sound dismissive and trite rather than interested and concerned.

Your Call Is Important to Us; Please Hold

Nearly every bank, huge corporation, and small business has shifted from human telephone operators to automated calling systems. Is that because, as businesses like to say, *Your call is important to us; please hold*? Or is it because it's less expensive to have a machine rather than a person deal with calls?

In the past, the automated system could be overridden, and the call could be directed to a person by hitting the 0 button; however, companies have learned that we're not stupid and have adjusted accordingly. Now, we usually have to listen to about twenty-five options before the option of talking to a person is given; then, the operator is usually so overloaded that over and over again, we get to hear *Your call is important to us; please hold*.

Stop insulting our intelligence by using that message. We know that we're just another customer and that, if we get annoyed, there are millions of others waiting behind us, probably listening to the same damn message.

11

Older Than Dirt
COMMON CLICHÉS AND
IRRELEVANT PHRASES

We all know that using clichés is an ineffective way to communicate; all of the little drops of wisdom have evaporated due to years and years of use. If there's an even less effective way to speak than using a standard cliché, then it's using a common expression that is so old and outdated that it no longer has any relevance.

If you have the brain power to remember all of these old, tired phrases, then you should have the ability to come up with something clever to say in your own words—at least every once in a while.

Ain't Ain't a Word, So Don't Use It

The phrase *Ain't ain't a word, so don't use it* has been around since at least the 1960s, so since we should all know by now that *ain't* isn't a word, we shouldn't use the phrase.

As Easy As Pie/Piece of Cake

What is the correlation between baked goods and something that's easy?

Both *as easy as pie* and *piece of cake* were more appropriate before baking from scratch meant slicing a piece of cookie batter from a prepackaged roll and tossing into a stainless-steel convection oven.

Back to the Drawing Board

Correct me if I'm wrong, but haven't computers replaced everything as the place to do our work? Perhaps we used to literally *go back to the drawing board* when we needed to start over on a project, but we don't now, and continuing to say so proves how out of touch we are.

Battle Lines Were Drawn

Battle lines were drawn is an outdated phrase that was used when wars were common and the country was filled with an us-versus-them mentality.

Come to think of it, it might not be outdated after all, and its sister phrase, *draw a line in the sand*, is more relevant than ever.

Beating a Dead Horse

Beating a dead horse shouldn't bring about the image of someone who doesn't know when to stop doing something; it should bring about the image of someone being arrested on charges of cruelty to animals.

Stick with more civilized phrases.

By the Skin of Your Teeth

Fine, maybe we don't all floss as much as we should, but do we need to keep talking about *skin* on our *teeth*?

By the skin of your teeth is a reference from the Bible, and unless we get back to using *thee*'s and *thou*'s in everyday language and having our children *begotten*, then it's probably time to find a new way to talk about a situation in which you barely escaped danger.

Cooking with Gas

Presumably, the expression *cooking with gas* came into being as a way of describing a process that was moving quickly and efficiently when gas stoves replaced wood stoves. In other words, this phrase has been outdated since 1912, which is when the electric stove was invented.

Discretion Is the Better Part of Valor

Discretion is the better part of valor is one of those phrases that we have said so often and for so long that we no longer question the authenticity of the statement. What if the fireman who had to make the choice about entering the burning building to try to save a child used that philosophy?

Simply stated: *Discretion* is simply **not always** *the best part of valor*, and the problem, which extends beyond this entry, is that an unquestioned acceptance of a phrase can lead to an unquestioned personal or societal belief.

Don't Count Your Chickens Before They Hatch

We have become so trained to repeat the same phrases over and over that many people who have never seen a farm, let alone a chicken farm, are spitting out the phrase *Don't count your chickens before they hatch*. It's said in meetings where millions of dollars are at stake, which would represent many hatched eggs. At home, even in concrete-filled cities, people are giving heartfelt advice by saying *Don't count your chickens before they hatch*.

It's the twenty-first century, and we're using a phrase that was appropriate when most of us raised our own food. Saying *Don't count your tattoos before the ink dries* would make more sense since more people have tattoos on their bodies than hens in their backyards.

Try that one on your boss in the next meeting.

Greatest Thing Since Sliced Bread

Since the automated bread slicing machine was invented in the 1920s, there have been many great innovations and achievements, including, but not limited to, the personal computer, the Internet, men on the moon, and the Chia Pet.

What is so special about a machine that slices through bread that we're still talking about *the greatest thing since sliced bread* eighty-plus years later? Was it that difficult to build a machine with sharp blades spaced half an inch apart? Besides, was slicing bread one of the most pressing needs in the 1920s? Perhaps people should have been paying more attention to the economy and stock market.

He Is His Own Worst Enemy

I understand that for many people, the biggest roadblock to becoming successful is often that they sabotage themselves in some way; however, one of the biggest roadblocks to being able to communicate more effectively is often the tendency to use an ancient phrase, such as *He is his own worst enemy*, rather than using fresh words.

Try *He needs to have more confidence* or *He always seems to say the wrong thing in an important situation* or something else relevant to the situation.

Hit by a Mack Truck

We all know how important advertising is to any product, and it's unfair that the biggest corporations often get free advertising. For instance, a cola is often generically referred to as a Coke; a tissue is often referred to as a Kleenex. Those corporations don't need free publicity.

That's why I think we should change the expression *Hit by a Mack truck* to *Hit by a Freightliner truck*. It's going to hurt just as much, but at least we'll be giving some publicity to a less-famous company.

Icing on the Cake

Every time I hear the phrase *icing on the cake*, I wonder who eats cake without icing. Sure, a pineapple upside-down cake or a strawberry shortcake might come without icing, but nearly every other cake arrives with icing.

The phrase is so old that it predates the time when *icing* was standard on a *cake*, so unless you think you can't buy a beer because of Prohibition, it might be time to put this phrase on ice.

If at First You Don't Succeed, Try, Try Again

If at first you don't succeed, try, try again; wonderful advice but a worthless phrase.

Any piece of advice that is given in the form of a cliché will be received in the way that it's given—old and worn out.

If It Ain't Broke, Don't Fix It

Even if we could pretend for a moment that it were ever acceptable to use the substandard word *ain't* in a sentence or that it should be *broken* and not *broke*, the phrase *If it ain't broke, don't fix it* has an even more basic flaw.

It's possible to fix only something that is broken; therefore, it is illogical to even talk about the possibility of *fixing* something that *ain't broke*. The phrase makes as much sense as talking about the possibility of driving a car from California to Hawaii.

The intention of the phrase is to say *If something is working in an acceptable manner, then we shouldn't waste our time trying to improve it.*

The phrase is what's *broken,* and instead of *fixing it*—just discard it.

I'm with You on That/
I'm Right There with You

It might be boring to always make the same comments in the same way day after day after day. That's why phrases such as *I'm with you on that* and *I'm right there with you* were invented to express agreement. The problem is that nontraditional phrases such as these get annoying quickly, but saying *I agree* doesn't. That's the beauty of boring—it may not be new, but it probably won't be annoying.

It's All Downhill from Here

It's hard to understand why the phrase *It's all downhill from here* is so often used as a reference to something negative, as in saying *It's all downhill from here* to someone who just turned forty. *It's all downhill* was originally intended to mean that the hardest part is over, which makes sense. And if you're unsure, then ask any marathon runner if he'd rather have the twenty-sixth mile be uphill or downhill. The phrase is probably confused with the common expression *to go downhill*, which means to deteriorate, as in *My golf game has gone downhill since I got new clubs.*

Because so many of us use the phrase incorrectly, none of us should use it at all.

It's as Easy as 1, 2, 3/A, B, C

Basic counting and memorization of the alphabet should remain part of the kindergarten curriculum, and *It's as easy as 1, 2, 3*, and *It's as easy as A, B, C*, should be removed from the vocabularies of all adults—unless, of course, the adults are singing the old Jackson Five song.

It's Like Trying to Find a Needle in a Haystack

A great number of people must sew while in the barn; otherwise, there would be no reason to continue using the antiquated expression *It's like trying to find a needle in a haystack.*

It's Not Exactly Rocket Science

It didn't *exactly* take a *rocket scientist* to tell me that the expression *It's not exactly rocket science* is ridiculously overused. In fact, this former meteorologist was bright enough to find more than 9,000 entries for the phrase in a recent Internet search, which, alone, gives an indication of its excessive use.

Before it reaches 10,000, we should blast it to Mars.

Knock on Wood

Am I the only person who has no idea of the origin of this phrase, what it means, and why we keep saying it? The only thing more annoying than saying *Knock on wood* is when someone says *Knock on wood* and sees nothing wood to knock on and then knocks on plastic and says *Make that knock on plastic.*

Last but Not Least . . .

The expression *last but not least* had its origins in the theater, and it was said so that the audience would understand that the last named actor or actress was not the least important. Presumably, the audience was bright enough to understand that without being told; it was probably done for the benefit of egotistical actors.

Nowadays, credits are preceded by the line informing us that the names of the actors are listed in order of appearance. Either that or the actors *are* actually listed in order of importance, which would actually mean that the last actor listed *was last and least.*

Let Me Put in My Two Cents

The expression *Let me put in my two cents* was basically intended to mean *Let me give you my opinion even though I understand that it might be of little value.* In the past—long past, that is—two cents was of little value and, as such, worth a tiny amount of consideration. Now, two cents is something that we wouldn't even bend over to pick up off the street, so unless that's the value of your opinion, don't use *Let me put in my two cents.*

Light as a Feather

Saying it's as *light as a feather* used to be an excellent simile, effectively painting a picture that the object in question didn't weigh much. Now that the number of times the phrase has been uttered has exceeded the number of feathers on all the birds on the planet, it effectively paints the picture of the author of a language book standing up and screaming: *Can't you think of something besides a feather to use as reference for something that is light!?*

Make a Mountain out of a Mole Hill

Unless you want to sound like Ma and Pa Kettle discussing the problems of mid-twentieth-century farm life in America, there are more contemporary ways of talking about the possibility of exaggerating a problem rather than by saying *making a mountain out of a mole hill*—like saying, for example, *stop exaggerating.*

Off the Charts

Off the charts became a popular phrase when selling records—you know, the round vinyl discs that would spin round and round—was the mark of success. Now that we've moved from records to eight-tracks to cassettes to compact discs and digital music, it might be time to record a new phrase.

Preaching to the Choir

The phrase *preaching to the choir* is as old as the Vatican itself, but that's only part of the problem. Choir members *have* to come to the service every week; perhaps it's not that they are seeking salvation but, rather, that they're interested in singing.

Now, it might be different if the phrase were *preaching to the couple in the front row who hasn't missed a service in thirty-four years.*

Put My/Your Best Foot Forward

It once took more than six months for my badly sprained ankle to completely heal. During that time, I did, in fact, have a *best foot* to *put forward* . . . and backward . . . and sideways. I may have had a temporary excuse to use this lame phrase, but there has to be a better way to talk about giving maximum effort.

Rome Wasn't Built in a Day

Whenever I hear the ancient expression *Rome wasn't built in a day*, it makes me think of the great philosophical question *Which came first, pasta or the Roman Colosseum?* Just kidding; actually, what I think is *Nothing is built in a day, so we need to find a new way of saying that we need to be patient.*

Six of One, Half a Dozen of the Other

Doughnuts and bagels!! That's all people ever think of when the expression *six of one, half a dozen of the other* is used. That's because doughnuts and bagels are two of the few things that we still purchase by the dozen. That wasn't the case when this phrase was first used—a hundred or more years ago.

Talk about being stale!

The Apple Doesn't Fall Far from the Tree

If you use the expression *The apple doesn't fall far from the tree* as a way of explaining that family members tend to have the same traits, then you may as well use it to describe yourself—since the expression was used by your parents and grandparents and great-grandparents.

Update it to a more modern fruit or vegetable: perhaps *The mango doesn't roll far in the grove* or *The asparagus doesn't fall far from the stalk.*

The Only Thing We Have to Fear Is Fear Itself

While the theory behind Franklin Roosevelt's much quoted *The only thing we have to fear is fear itself* line is understandable, in practice, it doesn't always apply. Ask a soldier standing across the desert from people who would like to kill him if his problem is *fear itself* or the weapons aimed at him.

Time Is of the Essence

Time is of the essence has become so trite from years and years of overuse that it no longer accurately communicates that time is of any consideration. In fact, the expression is so tired that the listener, out of a passive-aggressive protest, will probably slow down upon hearing it.

Tip of the Iceberg

In this age of air travel, one of the few times that most of us ever get into a ship is for a two-week tropical cruise where the closest thing to the *tip of the iceberg* is the top of the ice cube in our umbrella drink.

Nowadays, however, we use this phrase as often as we accumulate frequent flyer miles, which means that it's time for the phrase to be permanently defrosted.

Two Heads Are Better Than One

Two heads are better than one can be an accurate expression—unless you only have one hat.

Actually, in many instances, two people working together to solve a problem is, indeed, better than one person working alone; however, if *Two heads are better than one* is the most modern and articulate way of expressing that sentiment, then don't expect to solve the problem in a creative way.

Perhaps you'll need a stadium full of heads in order to get a fresh idea or two.

Two Wrongs Don't Make a Right

It's common knowledge that a double negative makes a positive when dealing with grammar; for example, *I have never not gone to Sunday service* means that *I've always gone to Sunday service.* However, no rational person ever believed that *Two wrongs made a right*, so why do we keep reminding everyone of that lack of logic?

Up in the Air

It must be getting crowded *up in the air*, with airplanes, helicopters, and satellites having to share space with so many people. It seems as though everyone were *up in the air* about one thing or another.

Where There's Smoke, There's Fire

It's common to use the cliché *Where there's smoke, there's fire* when someone is trying to explain that one thing follows the other in a predictable manner, but do we have to be so predictable when saying it?

You Can Attract More Flies with Honey Than with Vinegar

Of course, *you can attract more flies with honey than with vinegar*, but until someone tells me why I should want to attract flies, I'm going to stop talking about it.

In fact, I'm going to leave a jar of vinegar on my veranda—to repel as many flies as possible.

You Can Take That to the Bank

With ATMs (see entry in Chapter 2) and direct deposit of paychecks, most of us rarely *take* anything *to the bank* any longer, which means that we should try to find a new phrase for something that you can count on.

You Hit the Nail on the Head

You hit the nail on the head is one of those automatic response phrases that is given so often and in so many situations that it's pretty clear that the speaker is not thinking about what he's saying. In fact, it's often said in a shortened *You hit the nail* or changed to *You hit the nail on that one* out of pure boredom or because the speaker thinks that's more clever than the actual cliché.

Here's a suggestion: Engage in the conversation at hand rather than using pre-recorded thoughts.

12

Stop Playing Games
INEFFECTIVE SPORTS
TERMINOLOGY

In the past, the area of spectator sports was generally considered to be a part of pop culture; attending a sporting event could never rival theater or opera or perhaps even a movie as first-class entertainment.

As our society's culture has evolved into one in which pop culture has become mainstream, spectator sports has taken a much larger role. For example, Super Bowl Sunday has practically become a national holiday, and in many areas, attending a game is high culture; it's the thing to do.

Naturally, as this evolution has taken place, the role of sports and language has changed as well, and many references to sports have started to appear in everyday language. In almost all instances, however, sports references are either too informal or not understood well enough to be an effective way to communicate.

Sports words and phrases should be used *sparingly*, and I'm not talking about bowling.

Adversity

When a basketball player making $6,000,000 has a successful season after not playing for two seasons because of injuries, it's said by fans and the media that *He has overcome a lot of adversity*. When a baseball team with a payroll of $200,000,000 is struggling to make the playoffs because of distractions related to a dispute between the manager and the star player, fans and the media say that *This team is dealing with a lot of adversity*. When a football team performs below expectations because the star player didn't honor his contract because he wants to make more money, fans and the media say that *The team was not able to overcome adversity*.

With so many people having real *adversity*, is this how we really want to define the word *adversity*?

Coughed It Up/Picked It Off

It's only a matter of time until a mistake in everyday life will be referred to as having *coughed it up* or having been *picked off*. Sports references have shifted from the radio booth to the world at large too often for it not to happen again; now, football announcers refer to interceptions and fumbles by these terms more often than they use the words *fumbled* and *intercepted*.

We already say he *dropped the ball on that one* or that was *a fumble on his part* often enough, so it won't be long until a business owner who is beaten by his main competitor is said to have been *picked off* or when someone who burns dinner is told he *coughed it up*.

Cracking the Whip

I'm not sure if *cracking the whip* is a horse-racing phrase or, heaven forbid, left from the days of slavery. Either way, because of the obvious negative images it evokes, we desperately need a new way of saying that a person is becoming more demanding.

Don't Bet on/Against It

Don't bet on it and *Don't bet against it* are two of the most overused phrases in the entire English language, and it's time to leave them at the OTB window.

Don't Count Him Out

Most Americans don't like boxing; it's too violent. They love to use boxing phrases, though, and *Don't count him out* has had a longer career than George Foreman—including the grill.

Get It into High Gear

I'd never classified auto racing as a sport until I pulled a neck muscle while backing out of a parking spot in front of the grocery store. Now, just as I do before all of my sporting activities, I stretch before driving. I also consider my eighty-year-old aunt an athlete when she drives to bingo every Tuesday night.

Anyway, *Get it into high gear* is a cliché that shouldn't have survived the transition from all cars having manual transmissions to most cars having automatic transmissions since drivers now, for the most part, have limited control over which gear the car is in. Just hit the gas and let the car do the rest of the work.

Give 110/150/200 Percent

Giving anything more than 100 percent is physically impossible. While I understand that people who say *give 110 percent* or *150 percent* or *200 percent* are trying to exaggerate in order to make a point, it doesn't work since the phrase has spread from a few sports announcers to the entire English-speaking world.

Most of us only use only 10 percent of our brain power. Dig into the 11th percent and find another way to say that an *excellent effort has been made*.

Go the Extra Mile

Presumably, *go the extra mile* originated in the world of track and field as a reference for one of the long running events; however, at this point, it's as tired as a marathon runner on mile twenty-five.

Here's One for the Record Books

Some of the great sports records, such as Joe DiMaggio's fifty-six-game hitting streak in baseball, might last for generations, but sports fans like to believe that someday even the great records will be exceeded.

One record that might never be broken is the number of times people say, *Here's one for the record books.*

It's Going Down to the Wire

In the world of gambling, if something is *going down to the wire*, then it's going to be an exciting finish with the potential for a big payoff, especially in regard to a horse race. In other words, it's not something that would be expected to happen often. Logically, then, the phrase *It's going down to the wire* shouldn't be used in nearly every conversation.

It's Time to Hang It/Them Up

This cliché, which originated as an expression referring to a retiring athlete, as in *It's time for Brett Favre to hang up his cleats,* might be acceptable when referring to athletes since, symbolically at least, they have equipment to hang up when their careers end. Like any catchy phrase, it lost any semblance of cleverness when it started to be said almost as often as the thought it was trying to replicate.

Adding to the problem of overuse is that the phrase has spread into different areas of life. For example, is it really the same thing when Frank, an accountant, has a bad day at the office and comes home and says to his wife *I think it might be time for me to hang it up*? Is he going to bronze a pencil, mount it beside a calculator, and charge for autographs?

Knockout Punch

A left jab from the fifty-five-year-old business manager who is trying to *knock out* her competition is followed by a right hook by the eleven-year-old with thick glasses who is trying to *knock out* his competition in the science fair is followed by a quick left–right combo by the thirty-eight-year-old who is trying to *knock out* his opponent in the recreation league tennis tournament.

We're all swinging at everyone and everything, and the main loser is the English language, which is stuck with yet another phrase without any real punch.

Left to Go

Both sports announcers and fans fall into the trap of saying that there are *two minutes left to go* in the game. Use either *two minutes left in the game* or *two minutes to go in the game* rather than the repetitious *left* and *to go* since *left* already means *to go*.

Let the Chips Fall Where They May

I feel silly about having complained that auto racing is considered a sport (see "Get It into High Gear," earlier in this chapter) now that poker is treated like a sport; it's on sports television networks, and announcers analyze every move in the same manner in which they analyze a football game. At least with auto racing, the participants can't drink beer and smoke cigars until *after* the event.

Speaking of feeling silly, many of us, including me before looking in the *American Heritage Dictionary of Idioms*, believe that *Let the chips fall where they may* is a reference to poker; however, the reference has to do with flying wood chips while chopping wood. The fact that few of us probably realize we're talking about wood chips and not gambling should be enough of a reason to stop using this phrase.

Money Shot

Money shot is quickly becoming an expression that generally expresses performing well under pressure. The assumption is that it originated in the world of sports, and that may be true; however, without going into details, some people believe that *money shot* originated in the world of adult movies.

With that in mind, perhaps we want to think twice about adding that to our list of popular phrases!

Out of My/His/Her League

Nothing has ever been accomplished that wasn't first believed to be possible. Limiting yourself by saying that something (or someone) is *out of my league* doesn't make sense, but if you must, at least try to find an original way of placing those limits on yourself.

As far as putting *your* limits on someone else by saying *out of his league* or *out of her league*, it isn't something that you have the right to do, so stop trying.

Par for the Course

Even though the sports culture has become more popular, a large portion of the population doesn't use the phrase *par for the course* in a way that's consistent with its definition.

Par for the course means *what usually happens. Par* is the average score in golf. If a hole is a par four, then the golfer should be able to get the ball from the tee to inside the hole in four shots, and putting the ball in on the fourth shot is *par*. Do it in three shots, and you've shot one below par, which is good; thus low scores are better than high scores. Five or more shots is above par, which means that it might be time to take up tennis.

In common usage, however, *par for the course* is almost exclusively used in negative situations. For instance, if the baby got sick, it took twenty minutes to get through the line at the grocery store, a tire went flat on the way home, and you found three bills in the mailbox upon arriving home, we might hear a *That's par for the course* response.

Perhaps you have low expectations, so a bad day is what's expected. Because *par for the course* is almost always said in situations that are worse than average, however, people who don't know how to keep score in golf are confused about how to properly use the phrase. Consider me your language caddie. Leave this phrase at the clubhouse.

Perfect 16–0 Record

In the world of sports, words such as *great, amazing,* and *spectacular* are used to describe players, games, or particular plays more indiscriminately than a dentist says, "This might hurt a little." I'm not sure whether it's done because of the need to create the illusion of drama or whether the standards in sports are merely lower than in life, but I know that there is no need for the redundancy of a *perfect 16–0 record*.

The *16–0 record* already indicates that there has not been a loss, so the word *prefect* is not needed.

Put the Pedal to the Metal

Put the pedal to the metal can withstand the aforementioned problem with the transmission (see "Get It into High Gear," earlier in this chapter); however, merely the number of people who misuse this phrase should be enough for it to be removed from our collective vocabulary. Many people say *Put the pedal to the middle*, which might be fine if no one is in a hurry—but that's not the intended use of the cliché.

Raise the Bar

Every four years, during the summer Olympics, the number of people who know what *raise the bar* means increases a little. The track and field events are a pleasant distraction from the on-court and off-court action of the so-called dream team, USA basketball.

During the other three years, we should find another way of saying that we want to *raise expectations*.

Ready to Rumble

The next time that you even think about saying *Are you ready to rumble?* or *Let's get ready to rumble*, pause long enough to decide if you actually want to be known as a person who quotes the mottos of professional wrestling and boxing.

Step Up to the Plate

Step up to the plate, clearly a baseball reference, has become an extremely trite way of talking about *accepting a challenge* or *accepting responsibility*; however, we should all remember that a baseball player who succeeds at the plate (meaning gets a hit) three times out of ten is considered to be very successful.

Since we (I hope) have higher expectations of ourselves when we *accept new responsibilities or challenges*, our word choices should reflect those higher expectations.

Team Player

Being a *team player* is important for someone who's on a team and wants nothing but success for the team; however, the assumption that being a *team player* is always best or that everyone should strive to be a *team player* is limiting.

Albert Einstein wasn't a *team player*; Thomas Edison wasn't a *team player*; Bill Gates probably isn't a *team player*. Those fellows did pretty well for themselves. More often than not, people who work toward their own goals are happier and more successful than those who work for the goals of others.

There's Plenty of Time Left in the Game

It's ironic that people seem to say *There's plenty of time left in the game* only when the game is almost over and the outcome has almost assuredly been decided.

For example, in football, if the Steelers are leading the Jets by ten points at the beginning of the second half, then the announcers and fans never mention how much time is left in the game even though there is clearly *plenty of time left* for the Jets to overcome the deficit and win the game. Conversely, if that same situation occurs with only a minute and a half left to play, then the announcers and fans say *There's plenty of time left in the game.* They'd then explain a complicated (that is, impossible) series of events that would need to take place quickly in order for the Jets to win the game.

The reason this is done, of course, is that announcers want people to keep watching, and fans want to remain hopeful if their team is losing or don't want to get excited until the victory is ensured. It would be better, more realistic, and more accurate, however, to reserve any discussion about there being *plenty of time left* for when there is, in fact, plenty of time left and to find another way of saying that *Despite the limited time left, the outcome of the game is not yet certain.*

They Wanted It More Than We Did

The *They wanted it more than we did* line is more often used by fans than by players. Players occasionally use it during cliché-filled interviews, but with fans, it seems to be the explanation for every loss.

For the sports-obsessed fans whose happiness depends on the success of a sports team to the point that they speak in terms of *us* and *them* as though they were actually part of the team, it's less painful to blame a lack of effort rather than admit that their team wasn't as good as the opposition. In reality, though, professional athletes all want to win; otherwise, they would have never have risen to among the best in the world at their sport.

This Team Shows a Lot of Poise

This team shows a lot of poise—except for the spitting, the tobacco chewing, the sunflower seeds hanging out of their mouths, and the scratching of their private parts on national television. Sure, other than that, *this team* (and every other team) *shows a lot of poise*.

Up for the Challenge

When *up for the challenge* is used as a sports reference, it's typically reserved for athletes who are facing an extreme test, such as attempting to win a gold medal at the Olympics or trying to kick the game-winning field goal on Super Bowl Sunday.

In the non-sports world, where the rest of us live, the phrase is used more often than bookmarks at the Princeton Library, which renders it ineffective. Asking if a co-worker is *up for the challenge* of having a report done by Friday is like asking an All-Star pitcher if he's *up for the challenge* of pitching in his first spring exhibition game.

13

Write Your *Own* Book
MY PERSONAL LANGUAGE
PET PEEVES

There are many words, phrases, and expressions that should probably be avoided but that don't fit neatly into any of the previous chapters, so I lumped these into my personal pet peeves category. And since this is *my* book, here they are.

All right, I don't want to commit a lie of omission, so I'll admit that I stole—I mean borrowed—some of my wife's pet peeves as well. What can I say? We're both easily annoyed, and we like to talk about it. Think twice if you get a dinner invitation.

Back in the Day

So this new phrase is an old phrase minus the word *old* and a well-placed *s. Back in the old days* is what people have said for centuries. When was this *day* that so many people are talking about? This must have been some day. How 'bout *a long time ago . . .*

Boobs

Substituting the word *boobs* for breasts is the equivalent of using any number of off-color words to describe a man's penis—none of which will be mentioned here since those words, for some reason, have not been elevated to a level of social acceptance by the male-dominated society.

And that's *my* opinion—imagine how my wife feels about the degrading and insulting word!

To summarize, a *boob* is not a body part; it's a person who is an idiot. Either use anatomically correct words or don't say anything at all. As my wife suggests, point if you have to.

Chick Flick

We have enough *degrading terminology for women*—although *chick flick* is actually an equal-opportunity offender since it's also an offensive term for men.

As far as its reference to women, everyone knows that *chick* is a less-than-complimentary synonym for *female*, which makes it that much more degrading when women use it. Regardless, why do we stereotype anything that doesn't have guns, wars, or blood as something that only an emotionally weak, sensitive, intellectually inferior person—that is, a woman—would like? Didn't the word *macho* go out with the end of the big mustache and long, gold chains?

That's why *chick flick* is also an insensitive phrase for a man. Is it still considered emasculating in this society for a man to enjoy a movie that focuses on substance rather than bang? It must be—at least for people who continue to use the term *chick flick*.

Chill Out

Where did the expression *chill out* come from? What's wrong with saying *relax*? Maybe it comes from *cool off*, but we've decided that that isn't extreme enough.

Chill out reminds me a little too much of a night at the morgue.

Clicker

My wife would like to know: Why *clicker*? Ever heard of a *remote control*?

Comfort Zone

Comfort zone is used as a way of expressing that we're inside of our normal range of comfort, whether when partaking in a physical activity or when discussing an emotional or psychological state. It's often used with the understanding that we need to move out of that so-called *comfort zone* in order to improve ourselves. Today, though, *comfort zone* and *out of our comfort zone* are used merely as synonyms for *comfortable* and *uncomfortable*, which means that the phrase is quickly losing its original purpose.

I have an idea: Let's start by expanding our **language** *comfort zone* to include new phrases!

Crunch Time

Unless you're in a gym and it's time to do abdominal exercises, there are more articulate ways of expressing urgency than saying *It's crunch time*, including *This is an important time in the project* and *We need to get this done quickly* and *This is our last chance—we'd better get it right.*

By the way, adding *baby* at the end, as in *It's crunch time, baby,* only compounds the problem.

Disrespect

I'm waiting for Aretha Franklin to record a remake of her hit "Respect" with a *dis-* in front of it since using the word *disrespect* has increased tenfold since it's become fashionable to use it as a verb.

Technically, it was a verb in the seventeenth century, but it has rarely been used as a verb in our time. Our mothers were much more likely to say *Don't be disrespectful to your aunt* rather than *Don't disrespect your aunt.* In other words, it might technically be correct to use *disrespect* as a verb, but it's not accepted by all. Regardless, its main abuse is overuse.

That line is pretty good—Ms. Franklin is welcome to use it in the remake.

Diva

Our use of the term *diva* to refer to pop culture stars is yet another sign of our need for a culture of melodrama. It's hard to imagine that nearly every average singer who is fortunate enough to have a couple of successful songs is worthy of being labeled a *diva*, which in Latin means *goddess*.

Don't Get Caught with Your Pants Down

My wife wants to know whether underwear is included in the phrase *Don't get caught with your pants down*. There's already too much visual information given, and overall, it just evokes an image that I don't need in my head while I'm trying to hold a conversation with someone.

Besides, are there really that many instances in which you might find yourself without pants, especially in the business world, where this phrase is so often used?

Hunky Dory

Many of the entries in this book are here for only one reason—because they're said so often that their effectiveness has been lost. *Hunky dory* is not one of those phrases. It's not said that much, but this is one of those phrases for which once is more than enough—unless, of course, you're talking about David Bowie's *Hunky Dory* album.

I Love You/Her/Him to Death

I love you to death seems to be said right before we describe an unlovable aspect of the one we supposedly love so much, such as *I love my mother to death, but her nagging drives me crazy.*

There might be a better way of expressing the fact that we're not too happy with a loved one rather than saying something that sounds like a murder–suicide pact.

I'm Proud of You

There's a natural implication of superiority, at least in stature, when the phrase *I'm proud of you* is used. One person is secure, older, or more knowledgeable; the other is insecure, young, or a novice. It's appropriate for a parent *to be proud of* a young child; children need the adulation of an older, more competent, and trustworthy person to reassure them that they are on the right path.

It's completely inappropriate, though, for someone to *be proud of* a peer. Peers are on the same level, so using a phrase that lifts one above the other is condescending.

In that sense, it's inappropriate for anyone to be *proud of* a fully functional, healthy adult and say *I'm so proud of you* when the person has a special accomplishment. Adults are in control of their own lives; even though they might benefit from the support of other adults, there are better ways to express those sentiments, such as *That's quite an accomplishment* or *You must be proud of yourself.* Some of us think that the mentor–novice or teacher–student type of relationship might be an exception to this rule, but there is too much one-sided superiority for the phrase to be used by one adult to refer to another adult.

I'll be *proud of all of us* when we stop saying this!

Interface

As a noun, *interface* means a *common boundary between surfaces*, and as a verb, it refers to *communication between inanimate objects*, such as computers. Notice that neither as a noun nor as a verb does the word have anything to do with communication between two or more *people*.

Since we're not computers, we can't *interface* with anyone or anything.

I Told You So

Let's say that you turn the key on the used car that was purchased yesterday, and the engine grinds a couple of times and stops. No big deal. What car starts every time the key is turned? On the second attempt, the engine grinds and sputters, and a puff of black smoke rises from under the hood as it stalls. After a glance to see whether anyone is looking, you try it again. The engine chugs and chugs and chugs before finally starting.

As the confident smile of a person who made a good purchase fades, the engine falls out of the car, through the rusty frame, and leaves a huge divot in the driveway.

The next thing heard is the sound of a parent, sibling, spouse, significant other, or friend saying, *I told you so. I told you that car was a piece of junk. I told you not to buy a car from a man named Sal. I told you so.*

No one ever wants to hear *I told you so,* so don't say it—especially when you were correct.

It's a Good Investment

It's a good investment doesn't need to be banned; however, we do need to be careful how we use it.

Good ol' *Webster's* defines investment as (1) the "outlay of money for income or profit"; (2) "the sum invested"; or (3) "the property purchased." That means that, strictly speaking, an investment can be the actual process of spending money with the goal of making a profit. Investment can also be the money that is spent when trying to make a profit, whether proverbial shirts are lost or millions of dollars are gained. Finally, an investment can also be what was purchased with the money, whether that be a small piece of a company (stock) or a pair of shoes.

In our Wall Street–driven society since the 1980s, however, it seems that we typically think of *investment* as the first definition—the process of spending money with the goal of making a profit. A *good investment,* by our typical definition, is something that gains in value. Houses are usually *good investments.* As long as the house wasn't built on a buried toxic waste dump and is well maintained, it will be worth more when sold than when purchased. Depending on how the market goes and how well the company prospers, stocks may or may not be *good investments.*

An automobile, by that definition though, is typically not a *good investment.* It loses thousands of dollars in value the instant it is driven off the dealership's lot. It's the same thing with computers, furniture, and boats—unless they are collectors' items. We might be pleased to own them, and they may serve a good purpose; however, they're not *good investments* by our most common definition.

It's Tearing Me Apart

If there were a chapter on melodrama, then *It's tearing me apart* would be one of the main entries since it's melodramatic and overused.

If we were *all torn apart* every time someone said *It's tearing me apart*, then we'd all be emotional wrecks. It's used as a way of trying to sound more sincere than you actually feel. In reality, you're probably glad to be doing it—whatever it is. As my wife notes, saying *It's tearing me apart, but I have to break up with you* probably means that you're glad to be rid of the person.

Related phrases, such as *ripped my heart out, put my heart through a meat grinder, my whole world came crashing down,* and *turned my whole world upside down*, aren't any better—unless you're collecting possible titles for an upcoming country and western album.

I Worked My Butt/Ass Off

To be tactful, *I worked my butt off* or *I worked my ass off* is classless. At the very least, it brings about an unpleasant visual image, which, by the way, has nothing to do with work and, to be honest, makes the speaker seem as though he or she had no idea how to communicate in an appropriate manner.

If it were said only in the most informal situations, then it might not be a problem—friends often say things to each other that they'd never say in a more public arena—but that's not the case. This phrase has spread into everyday life. I hear it said at work, in the grocery store, and at dinner parties.

It should never be said again—unless the conversation is about hard work at the gym and the reduction of the gluteus maximus muscle into a gluteus minimus muscle.

Keep Your Options Open

The sentiment behind *Keep your options open* is valid, but the phrase is used too often to be articulate. Besides, are *options* something that *open* and *close*? That sounds more like something for a window or door. It makes more grammatical sense to *Consider your options* or to *Rule out an option* than it does to open or close them.

Lessen

For some inexplicable reason, the awkward word *lessen* has replaced the more appropriate words *diminish* and *reduce* in nearly all instances by nearly all people. For weather forecasters, winds *lessen* rather than *diminish*. The storm *lessens* in intensity rather than *diminishes* in intensity. For anchormen, a decrease in bus fares will *lessen* the impact of an increase in subway fares, and the president's economic plan will *lessen* the tax burden on the rich. For the average shopper, coupons *lessen* the cost of groceries.

As my wife says, is it that difficult to remember the words *diminish* and *reduce*?

Lose Weight While You Sleep

If we could only get the marketers who create commercials for late-night television to work on the real problems of the world rather than filling us with false hope. . . .

First, it was the $40 grill that would replace the oven, microwave, toaster, and all pots and pans and allow healthful meals for the entire family to be prepared in twenty-five minutes or less. Then, it was the abdominal equipment that would give you a six-pack in seven sweat-free minutes per day—by the way, that six-pack has nothing to do with beer.

Now, it's the magic pill that will allow you to *lose weight while you sleep*. If that were true, then the advertisers would have to warn you that by sleeping late on the weekend, you might awaken on Monday morning as a ninety-eight-pound weakling.

My Head Is Going to Explode

We all get frustrated when *We lose focus because there's too much activity going on around us* or when *We're having a difficult time solving a complicated problem* or any other number of situations, but the fact that so many of us immediately choose the expression *My head is going to explode* is a sign that we depend way too much on cookie-cutter phrases rather than on our ability to choose our words.

It's ineffective; it's unoriginal; it's inane; and it's melodramatic. In fact, when I hear it, I think *My cranium is going to go kaboom!*

My Team Always Loses When I Watch/ Go to the Game

It's little wonder that no Philadelphia sports team has won a championship since 1984; the city is littered with people who, by their mere presence at the game—or by sitting in front of a television during a game—cause the team to lose. It's not just Philadelphia fans, though, or else we could blame the cheesesteak.

This mysterious, negative game-influencing ability is an epidemic. Some of the more powerful fans can affect the game from great distances; from halfway across the globe, if they turn on the game, their team will lose. Ask them, and they'll practically brag that *My team always loses when I watch the game.*

The most powerful minds in the world are being wasted on sports. What a shame.

On a Daily Basis

My wife believes that *on a daily* basis is an example of our culture of drama; all you need to say is *daily* or *every day*.

She's right. Using more words doesn't make it sound more important; it just makes you sound more dramatic.

On So Many Levels

What is the difference between *It's wrong* and *It's wrong on so many levels*? No one ever explains these mysterious different *levels*; they must mean that *It's wrong for so many different reasons*, and, at the risk of stating the obvious, *reasons* are different from *levels*.

Out

There is a trend in the world of home improvement to combine the word *out* with a word that denotes action. *Paint out the wall* has started to replace *Paint the wall*; *Change out the light fixtures* has started to replace *Change the light fixtures* or *Replace the light fixtures*; *Build out the bookcase* has replaced *Build the bookcase*.

Obviously, the *out* is not needed in these phrases, and it's a habit that we don't want to get *into*.

Quality Time

Back in the day—I mean, when I was young—we didn't have the phrase *quality time*. In recent decades, however, it has emerged as a reference for special time spent with children. The only logical conclusion is that children of today need special time with parents more than did children of the past—wait, that's not logical.

Children spend too much time alone for reasons that are both avoidable and unfortunate: in front of televisions and computers, in day care with strangers, alone in their rooms, or with one parent because of a divorce. Rather than trying to pretend that three minutes with a child is equal to three hours, if we emphasize the importance of the activities chosen during the shorter period of time, it might be better to find a way to spend more time with our children.

Real Deal

He's the real deal or *They're the real deal* or *It's the real deal* is a way of trying to express that a person, group of people, or a thing is legitimate in some way. Perhaps the person is an athlete who is destined for greatness or it's a business opportunity that will most certainly earn millions.

Irony might be the true *real deal* in this case since it's ironic that people would try to explain greatness in a trite way. It's parallel to describing Michael Jordan's career as average.

Recreate

While *recreate* is a verb, there are less confusing ways to say *to take recreation*, especially since we have also started to use the prefix *re-* with the word *create* without the necessary hyphen in order to say that we *created something again*.

In other words, because of our hesitancy to use a hyphen correctly, we now have two identical words that mean two different things, so it's now best to avoid both unless you're going to use the hyphen correctly, especially in writing, where the words can be confused.

The Big O and Whether Size Matters

Part of the reason for the always-popular base humor is that it is base. We're not supposed to talk about sex, so base jokes are an opportunity for comedians or advertisers to be bold and shocking and for the rest of us to prove that we're not prudish. It says something about our society that some base jokes have been overused to the point of becoming trite.

That's certainly the case with jokes about women having an orgasm and the size of a man's penis. There is now a website that sells furniture, clothing, and housewares, and their main advertising premise is *the O*; it's hard to understand why, other than they like to say, *It's all about the O*. In fact, the nickname *Big O* has pretty much replaced the word *orgasm* altogether.

As far as length not being a concern, the length of time you sit and watch football doesn't matter because you're virtually guaranteed that you'll see at least one commercial that uses the phrase *Size doesn't matter* or *It turns out that size does matter* during the first commercial break. The advertising ploy is used for any number of ridiculous products. It turns out that *Size does matter* when buying a car, so if you have a family of six, you might not want to buy a two-door with no backseat.

Popular—meaning pop culture—magazines might be worse. Try to find one magazine without at least one reference to whether size does or doesn't matter. In most instances, it's the witty headline that the crack editor came up with, such as *Size Doesn't Matter* for an article about car mufflers or *Size Does Matter* plastered above an article about portion size and weight loss.

I don't know about you, but now that we understand that women have orgasms and men have penises of different sizes, can we move on?

Veggie, Carb, and Cammie

If I were writing an entire book on my wife's pet peeves, then abbreviating words for no legitimate reason would be section one of chapter one, and the topic might spill into additional chapters.

As she likes to say, "Doesn't the original word accurately say what we want to say? Why did we have to make up *veggies* for *vegetables* or *carbs* for *carbohydrates* or *cammie* for *camisole?* I could go on." (Believe me, she could.)

Are we trying to be cute? We don't call a sofa a *sof.* Is it too difficult to say the extra syllable or two?

War on Terror

Terror is being afraid to live your life; it's a threat of violence or danger; it's fear to the point of being paralyzed. It's not something tangible; it's being afraid. In other words, *terror* is an idea or a concept or an emotion, and I wish I could tell you how many times over the past several years I've heard my wife say to the television *You can't have a war on terror; terror is an idea. You can't have a war on an ideology because you can't kill an ideology—at least not with guns and bombs.*

Frankly, she's right. You cannot have a *war on terror* any more than you can have a *war on panic.* If you have a war against a particular country, when that government is removed from power, the war is over. You can have a *war on terrorists;* however, if these terrorists are not represented by a single government or are spread out across several countries, there will be no way to know when the war has ended or how successful it's been.

We need to make sure that we have a clear definition of phrases when they are used as a reason to execute military action, and a *war on terror* is not possible.

We're Pregnant

We're pregnant may not be as graphic as *We're trying to have a baby* (see next page), but it's also less accurate. Say that to my wife, and she'll respond with, "Really? You're both pregnant? The magic of modern medicine!"

Try *We're expecting* rather than the biologically impossible version in which the man is pregnant, too.

We're Trying to Have a Baby

Do you know what people think when they hear *We're trying to have a baby*?

I'll give you a hint: They don't think about the stork dropping a little bundle on the front steps. They think about you having sex—often. They think they know why you were fifteen minutes late for work; they think they know why you didn't answer the door when both cars were in the driveway; they think you were lying when you said you were out of breath because you were on the treadmill when you answered the telephone.

It's hard to imagine a reason to share such personal information, but if it must be done, then try saying, *We're hoping to start a family soon.* Just stop saying that *We're trying to have a baby.*

What Did You Watch Last Night?

Some words or phrases should be avoided not because of what they actually say but, rather, how they might reflect on the speaker. That's the case with asking *What did you watch last night?* Asking this question lets everyone know that you watch television every night and that you assume that everyone else does as well.

What did you do last night? would be a less presumptuous question—and less telling.

Wow Factor

There are already a million ways to say that something has that *je ne sais quoi*, which, for those of you who don't have a spouse who speaks French, basically means *a certain something that's hard to describe*. Why do we have to invent yet another inarticulate phrase—*wow factor*—when there are more specific words that already exist, such as *dazzling* and *exciting* and *has panache* and *is colorful*?

Seriously, if *wow factor* is the most descriptive phrase you can generate, then the only thing that people are going to be saying *wow* about is your poor vocabulary.

You Guys

It's almost impossible for a group of two or more people, regardless of gender, to be served in a restaurant—even so-called fine dining establishments—without being called *you guys* at least six times. Nothing takes the elegance out of a formal or intimate dinner more quickly than informal service, and in case it's escaped everyone who works in the service industry, 51 percent of us are not *guys*.

The overuse of the phrase, which is a symptom of pop culture becoming mainstream, is not limited to restaurants. Anywhere a service is provided—stores, doctors' offices, and opera house box offices—men, women, boys, and girls are all generically referred to as *guys*. It won't be long until *guys* replaces *sir* and *madam* as the reference of choice in retirement homes—if it hasn't already.

INDEX